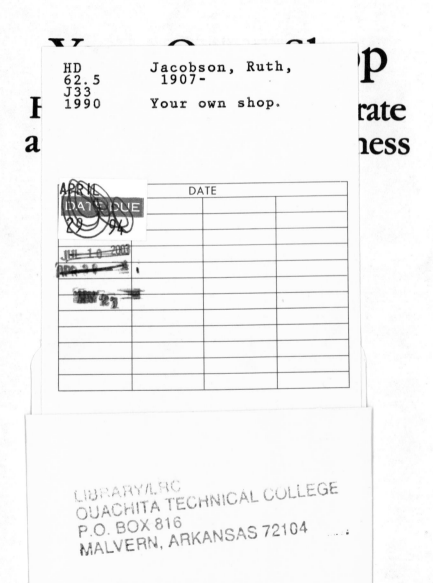

DATE		
DATE DUE		

BAKER & TAYLOR BOOKS

In memory of Harry Jacobson
my husband, my friend, my mentor

Your Own Shop
How to Open and Operate a Successful Retail Business

Ruth Jacobson

LIBERTY HALL
PRESS™

LIBERTY HALL PRESS books are published by LIBERTY HALL PRESS, an imprint of McGraw-Hill, Inc. Its trademark, consisting of the words "LIBERTY HALL PRESS" and the portrayal of Benjamin Franklin, is registered in the United States Patent and Trademark Office.

FIRST EDITION
SECOND PRINTING

© 1991 by LIBERTY HALL PRESS, an imprint of McGraw-Hill, Inc.

Library of Congress Cataloging-in-Publication Data

Jacobson, Ruth, 1907-
Your own shop : how to open and operate a successful retail business / by Ruth Jacobson.
p. cm.
Includes index.
ISBN 0-8306-3466-5 (paper)
1. New business enterprises. 2. Retail trade. I. Title.
HD62.5.J33 1990   90-40307
658.8'7—dc20   CIP

For information about other McGraw-Hill materials,
call 1-800-2-MCGRAW in the U.S. In other countries
call your nearest McGraw-Hill office.

Vice President and Editorial Director: David J. Conti
Book Editor: Marie Bongiovonni
Production: Katherine G. Brown
Book Design: Jaclyn J. Boone

Contents

Part IV   Structuring and Funding the Business

Part V Appendices

Acknowledgments

I take this opportunity to express my thanks to the members of my family. My profound indebtedness to my daughter Natalie Jacobson McCracken, editor at Boston University, who edited the manuscript before it went to the publisher and made the final preparations for publication; Sam McCracken, who provided the computer services that readied the manuscript for the typesetter; Harry McCracken, who is responsible for the information on computers and their value to small business; Elizabeth McCracken, who did the research regarding the marketing of the book; Carolyn and Norman Matulef, for their enthusiasm and encouragement; my sister Blanche Bernstein, for her perceptive appreciation.

I am particularly grateful to Craig Rice, author of numerous business books, for invaluable advice on getting the book published. My thanks go to Sol Davidson, business counselor, and Martin Zober, professor emeritus at the University of Iowa, both of whom read the manuscript and provided illuminating observations.

My very special thanks go to David J. Conti, editorial director of Liberty Hall Press, who provided me with the opportunity to share my entrepreneurship with a reading public, and Ellen Greenberg, a text editor who improved immensely my style of presentation.

To the reader

PLANNING FOR THE SUCCESSFUL START AND OPERATION OF A RETAIL STORE IS THE theme of this book. It is not a theoretical study, nor does it contain a single statistical compilation. It does not offer a magical formula. It is a practical plan for establishing and operating the store of your choice. In non-technical language it addresses the sophisticated needs of today's merchant.

The book fills a unique role because it is written for the retail entrepreneur; even more specifically, it is for you, the newcomer in the field. Its purpose is to transform your dreams into reality by providing you with the necessary basic information for getting started, and then continuing to operate with a profit.

Shopping is a national pastime. Because we are all retail customers, in and out of shops almost daily, it may seem easy to start such a business—rent a storeroom or clear a corner of the living room, hire a part-time clerk and inveigle the spouse to do the bookkeeping. There follows the delightful experience of "going to market" to choose the merchandise at wholesale prices. Should you spend almost all of your working capital in this buying spree, "not to worry," you tell yourself, believing the money will come back twofold when store doors open to eager customers, checkbooks in hand.

This reverie, you may find out to your chagrin, is not an exaggeration: It is a simplified description of many who plunge into store ownership. They create the bankruptcy statistics of the unprepared.

Statistics tell us that within a year fifty percent of all new businesses are gone, and within ten years, ninety-five percent. The number of retail store closings is among the highest of the fatalities because they are the easiest businesses to open. There is no need for you to be among these statistics.

Instead of being discouraged by the preponderance of failures, learn how to be a successful survivor. Prevention is better than the cure, and cheaper. Beat the odds by knowing not only the answers but also the questions.

Today's small store is a miniature of the largest stores in your area and those more distant. Even the mail-order catalogs of the giants in your industry are among your competitors. The methods of operation of the small store must meet the challenge.

The "mom and pop" stores judged profit—or loss—by subtracting the total of invoices on the desk spindle from the money in the cash box and bank account. And the number of such unpaid spindled invoices was minimal—business with the suppliers was often "cash and carry." There was little advertising and frequently no payroll. Today the thought of starting and operating a business can be overwhelming—there is so much to know and to do. Business is hazardous—it has its risks. Business is also exciting, challenging, and there are ample examples of success in the retail business world. Risks can be minimized.

To head off failures and sail head-on to success is the lesson emphasized throughout this book. It's not merely a matter of strategy, which somehow implies "tricks of the trade." It's to know what's involved and to make plans accordingly—to anticipate potential problems and methods for solving them, to anticipate your strengths and know how to utilize them.

When my husband, Harry Jacobson, expanded the family business from a men's store to a department store, I became his partner. Harry was a great teacher and a patient one: his method was to let me learn from my own mistakes—costly but unforgettable lessons. His business standards were high: quality merchandise, services such as "The Big Store" offered, integrity as reflected in both customer and supplier relations, and firmly kept civic and community responsibilities.

Ten years after becoming a businesswoman I was widowed, and then I discovered how little I really knew about the financial operation. Luckily the coasting period of an established business stood me in good stead, and Jacobsons of West Des Moines continued as a successful business.

Twenty years later I closed the store and became a business counselor for the Service Corps of Retired Executives (SCORE), a volunteer adjunct of the U.S. Small Business Administration (SBA). I did eye-to-eye counseling and presented seminars. I was appointed executive director of the national SCORE office in Washington, District of Columbia, where I was involved in its nationwide program of business counseling; one of my assignments was to supervise the writing of counseling brochures. These experiences of working both locally and nationally with entrepreneurs in a wide variety of businesses, augmented by the wealth of counseling materials I had prepared, SBA made me ready for the next step, which was to become an independent business counselor.

I felt that I could be useful to both men and women retail entrepreneurs by sharing my own learning-by-doing experiences. This book should be useful not only for the newcomer in business, but also for the business counselor, and as a reference source for progress and the growth years of an ongoing business. Step by step, from start-up to day-by-day operation, the process is developed.

The introduction, Planning for Success, points out the importance of the well-planned retail store.

Part I: Entering the World of Retailing describes the qualifications for successful entrepreneurship, how to start a retail store from scratch or to buy an ongoing store, targeting the customers, as well as selecting the location and the building.

Part II: Charting a Successful Store Operation explains the role of the owner-manager, hiring and training employees, salesmanship, store policy, interior layout, and advertising media, along with buying and controlling store inventory.

Part III: Financial Recordkeeping and Analysis is about bookkeeping and accounting, cash flow, budget; and it provides rule-of-thumb tests of the store's profitability.

Part IV: Structuring and Funding the Business deals with insurance; the legal structure—sole proprietorship, partnership, corporation; financial planning—your money needs and resources for getting funds; drawing up your own business plan and updating it when ready for expansion.

The **Appendices** explain the uses of a computer system in retailing and contain a dictionary of business terms.

All of this information tells you not only what to do, but how to do it. And the effort that you put into learning how to be a successful entrepreneur will be surpassed by gratifying rewards—I promise you that.

Good luck as you open *Your Own Shop*.

Planning for success

THE TRIAL-AND-ERROR METHOD CAN PROVIDE NEVER-TO-BE-FORGOTTEN LESSONS, but it's wasteful of time and money that are both in short supply for the new shop owner. The results of "reinventing the wheel" could well be disastrous.

Someone once said, "Experience is a hard teacher because she gives the test first, the lesson afterwards." Of course we learn from failures. My first order of house slippers for my shoe department was my best—and bitterest—lesson in shoe buying. I bought every style that I selected in every single size. Failing to take into consideration the salable shoe sizes of my customers played havoc with my shoe department budget for a long, long time. Hindsight became foresight in future planning.

Look before you leap

Why gamble? Gamblers take risks based on chance. Planning by the store owner removes much of the risk. It is based on data research and experience as you, the business-manager-innovator-finalizer, study your own finances and the needs of your kind of business as you apply your own good judgment.

The secret of success is good management, and good management starts with careful planning. Planning saves time and money and eliminates errors before they occur. "Pencil and paper" errors are correctable by the eraser on the end of the pencil.

Business experts agree that the main cause of business failure is poor management. Therefore, in the final analysis of the small store, one must look directly to the boss to maintain advantages available to the small business. The boss must be a good manager, and good management not only starts with careful planning but must be followed by constant supervision of every area of operation to make sure the plan is followed.

My purpose is to help you see the whole picture before you make a single commitment. In this book, the step-by-step process of opening a store is developed. As you follow the planning process for your own store, you will be creating the potential of a prosperous future. When you reach the book's final chapter you will be able to construct a business plan that will help you establish reasonable objectives and will serve as a guide to success throughout your business's life.

The advantages of the small store

What are the chances of survival of a small retail store faced with competition from big business? "The Big Store" has prime location, eye-catching display windows facing heavily pedestrian-trafficked sidewalks, a large array of merchandise, full-page newspaper ads, colorful television promotions, and delivery service—which seems like a lot to overcome.

Now visualize the number of retail stores in the shopping malls and the retail stores that line the commercial strips of cities. Their biggest advantage over "The Big Store" is personal service. It is because of the very personal nature of the small store that it can hold its own and even go beyond that. "The Big Store" cannot provide this relationship except in a watered-down, artificial presentation by employees who lack the owner's incentive. In a small store, whenever the customer enters the premises, he meets not only the boss but the same salesperson; the customer feels that the owner knows and appreciates the business relationship.

The owner knows the merchandise—he deals directly with the supplier and often the manufacturer. The same nationally known brands of merchandise are almost always as available to him as to the buyer of "The Big Store." He has particular customers in mind when buying the product. He has concern for the customer whether buying merchandise for stocking the shelves, selling it to the customer, or handling any complaints the customer may voice. And because it does not need a large share of the market, which "The Big Store" must have, the small store can operate capably with a share of profits inadequate for the large establishment.

High overhead has forced the giants in industry to cut sales forces to a minimum, to reduce the service that promotes comfortable and confident shopping. The fact that it can be more capital-efficient gives the small store an advantage.

This is where the small store comes into its own. Properly managed, the small store can establish itself as a fixture in its own neighborhood—easily accessible and offering prompt and "caring" service. This explains the success of the quick-trip food shops, where higher prices and limited stock have not been a deterrent.

The very personal nature, friendly and helpful, of the small store is its strength. The store owner knows the business in its entirety because he is responsible for all of it. He devotes personal attention to all phases of the business. Putting in a quick telephone call to the supplier when stocks run low, formulating the policy to meet changing situations, the owner reports only to himself and can act immediately when a situation arises. In a large business such decisions require top official approval—maybe even a meeting of its board of directors.

And even though there are areas where the storekeeper may lack complete confidence in himself at first, there is the personal satisfaction of achievement when, getting advice from no one but himself, he makes correct decisions and surmounts obstacles. He is his own helping hand.

The venture becomes an adventure

Greater than the risk in starting a store are the potential rewards of a well-managed store. There are risks in taking a new job, and getting wealthy working for someone else is almost impossible.

There are rewards particularly when you choose a business you enjoy—flowers, books, high fashion apparel, antiques. There is no monotony in the retailer's business day.

You have the satisfaction of having accomplished success by yourself. The diversity of retail store involvements—merchandising, salesmanship, advertising, finance, accounting, public relations—all become a widening vista of opportunities for creativity and initiative for you, the boss. You are the owner of the store.

Part I
Entering the world of retailing

1

Entrepreneurship —Is it for you?

CONFIDENCE IN YOUR OWN SPECIAL ABILITIES, THE PRODUCTS YOU PLAN TO sell, and the market's need for your kind of business give you motivations for success and self-assurance that there's a place in the business world for YOU.

What it takes to be a successful entrepreneur

Competence

Business experience and education are important assets when considering becoming a storekeeper, but personality-related qualifications are even more important. No matter how eager you are to have your own store, incompetence on your part can end only in business failure. More businesses fail because of poor management than for any other reason.

When you apply for a job, the employer analyzes your qualifications and capabilities. You must be equally objective when you analyze yourself—no alibis, no over-rating.

Competence involves good organization, ability to handle responsibility, willingness to work hard, perseverance, and decision-making ability. Sincerity, honesty, initiative, leadership that inspires confidence—all are personality requisites for successful retail store management.

Motivation

Motivation is the adrenaline which bolsters your answer to the question of why you want to go into business for yourself. Your motive may go back to childhood, when you envied the person behind the candy counter. Your motive may be financial gain and security if you've been unable to get a lucrative job. It may be that a certain kind of business appeals to you because of your particular abilities. You have confidence that you would be a successful fabric shop owner because of your ability to design and make clothing, and your college degree was in that field.

Perhaps you want to be your own boss to have control over your future. You may need a career that will fit in with family responsibilities—to set your own schedule and work arena.

In other words, motives fall into categories of independence, permanence, and investment—all worthwhile goals. However, you must ask yourself whether operating a retail store will answer these needs. The pleasure of financial security as a motivation should be measured against the profit if the same money were invested otherwise, while you drew a salary working for someone else.

Risk-taking

Successful store operation requires long hours, hard work, sacrifices—all because of the joy that the undertaking brings. The minuses of owning one's own business are the pluses of a job with someone else. As a storekeeper, initially you have to be there; delegation of responsibility to others comes later. At first, you can't call in sick or take vacations. Often you cannot leave the store for even one minute—there is no one there to take your place. The hours are long and often worrisome. But working for someone else, at the end of the day you usually leave the business and the worries behind.

In opening the business you risk your own money and your credit rating. You risk the money that you borrow. For the first month or perhaps even the first year, profits may be minimal.

If you have a spouse, capital that you intend to use as start-up funding may not be yours to use—it may be shared property, and perhaps not even that. Furthermore, you may not have established your own credit rating.

Liking people

High on the list of important qualifications for managing a store is liking people. There must be a personal relationship between owner and customer—not a social, but a friendly one—and a concern for the customer's needs, taste, and convenience. The old policy that the customer is always right endures—in fact, it has become even more important. The self-help set-up of big stores cutting down on salary expense gives added advantage to the small store and its owner, who is the buyer-salesperson-manager. Primarily, the owner-manager must be available to customers even if it entails doing stockwork and bookkeeping before or after store hours. Store hours are for the convenience of the customer and not the owner. Availability to the customer determines opening and closing hours.

Education and experience

To decide whether to go into business, consider also your business education, formal and informal, and business experience, particularly as it relates to the business you are considering. Don't underestimate the educational value of part-time jobs you held while in school—clerking in a clothing store during summer vacations, or even making hamburgers in a fast food shop, where you learned how to make change and handle a cash register.

Business education can be augmented in seminars sponsored by area colleges, universities, the chamber of commerce. The SBA and its volunteer affiliate SCORE offer classes and free publications that cover every area of business operation. Their local and area offices are listed in your telephone book.

The woman storekeeper

A woman often is faced with determining whether she can fit business ownership and operation with home responsibilities without either suffering. She must be able to handle long business hours along with the demands of a family. It may even require that she have a supportive family, with members who will relieve her of some household duties.

A career woman usually wears both hats—that of homemaker and that of business executive. A 1985 Boston University study indicated via some interesting statistics that the female married parent spends eighty-five hours a week on her job, homemaking, and child care, and a single female parent spends seventy-five hours on the same. Storekeeping might be even more time consuming.

Women are prone to underrate their business experience. For women particularly, volunteerism often provides business experience and education—serving as treasurer for a nonprofit organization or as merchandise buyer for a hospital guild gift shop. Homemakers' responsibilities and experiences encompass many areas of business operation. As family shoppers, their constant relationship with retail business prepares them for appreciation of standards for business management.

Women generally face their needs to prepare for going into business by attending classes provided for that purpose.

Filling the gaps in your knowledge

The prospective storekeeper might take a temporary or part-time job in a like business, working evenings or weekends if he has another job. He might study the business of competitors, walking through their stores and studying their merchandise, display methods, and advertising. Talking to business owners in neighborhoods other than your own, in other cities, can be worthwhile. There are books in the public library on every area of acquiring and operating a business. If there is an SBA office in your city, it can provide you with free brochures on every area of small business.

Your own qualification shortcomings may be corrected by taking a partner who has the work experience or the bookkeeping knowledge you lack, and even additional capital. You could hire a manager who has the necessary abilities, and offer him or her a share of the profits as an incentive.

Choosing your business

Choose the business that is right for you, one in which you are likely to succeed. No matter how great its potential may be for someone else, it must be right for you. It is fairly easy to start a small retail store, but it is difficult and expensive to get out of it. The crucial decision is yours.

The kind of business you choose should appeal to you, and confidence in the product and enthusiasm for the store operation are important. You want to enjoy every aspect of storekeeping. But your confidence and enthusiasm must be well-founded. The store's suitability for you depends upon a combination of your own abilities, what you are looking for in a business, and the business factors themselves.

What the business requires of you

A retail storekeeper should have those personality traits and store-management abilities applicable to all entrepreneurs, but more specifically those abilities, skills, and talents relating to the particular business under consideration. They relate even to your own lifestyle, hobbies, and interests. A garden shop is a seasonal business in many areas of the country—it is not for you if your interest is in a business that is active throughout the entire year, but it's an excellent choice if you welcome time-off periods. If golf, skiing, and tennis are among your personal activities, you might consider a sporting goods shop.

How do your experience and education apply to this particular store you are considering? If they've been in the area of carpentry, then building supplies or hardware are likely zones of your expertise. If your college degree was in home economics, a fabric shop, a clothing store, or an art needlework store would be viable businesses.

Funding

Consider the capital requirements of the business. Can you afford it? For a store that requires expertise relating to its products, the staff payroll may have to be taken into consideration, for salespeople who draw more than a minimum wage. Some merchandise requires more investment than others; for example, automobiles versus bicycles. Some storerooms are larger and therefore more expensive; the candy store versus the variety store.

If the items in your store are new on the market, you must be able to afford to create the market. Large corporations spend a long time and considerable money before launching a new product. Can you afford such waiting time and money? One of my clients had an exciting, marketable product, but its manufacturing and patenting costs ate up all of his capital. And by that time a comparable item, much less expensive, was on the market.

Unless you have had experience in that kind of business, justifying your self confidence, don't buy an ongoing store that is losing money.

Know the business. Know the merchandise. Don't go in cold. Don't buy a drugstore if you aren't a pharmacist unless you are mighty confident of a pharmacy staff.

Know the current outlook for this type of business and its future. An expanding market may justify your establishing a store in the same area as another like business. Don't be fearful of competition. It often strengthens the market. One antique store might be more profitable in an area with many antique stores, where customers can find them.

Know all about it

Know the products you stock. Know the business of selling that stock. Get your education before you go into business, not afterward.

Where do you go for suggestions of possible business opportunities? Turn to the classified ads in your newspaper, to the yellow pages of the telephone book, shopping malls, and commercial strips. Visit the public library for business dictionaries such as the *Thomas Register*, entrepreneural magazines, and consumer reports published by the government.

What you require of the business

The store you choose should satisfy your reason for going into business. You may be looking for security; as an employee you may have been threatened by layoff or early retirement. To allay such fears, consider the economic future and growth potential of this particular kind of business. A business that depends on the sale of a fad item or a store in a location without stability lacks the security you are seeking.

You may be looking for a store that will give you personal satisfaction—one that answers your desire to express your creativity, the independence that enables you to make your own decisions. You may be looking for a business that will give you more time with your family. Is wealth your goal, or the stability of a safe investment? These are all fundamental to a happy and successful business future, and determine what kind of store you want to own and operate.

A genuine business opportunity

It must be a profitable business with a future—in other words, a good current and developing market. Make an accurate study of economic trends and forecasts, the outlook for this kind of store. Review consumer reports that evaluate products you are considering selling. Study the rate of merchandise turnover in such a business and potential return on your investment of time and money. Profit is the bottom line. A spectrum of small retail businesses is listed in Fig. 1-1.

Antiques	Hobby shops
Art supplies	Household appliances
Art needlework	Ice cream
Baked goods	Jewelry
Bicycles	Kitchenware
Boutiques	Lamps
Boys' clothing	Liquor and wine
Building materials	Luggage
Candy	Magazines and newspapers
Cheese	Men's clothing
Children's clothing	Musical instruments
Convenience food stores	Paint and wallpaper
Crafts	Pianos and organs
Drugstores	Photography supplies
Fabrics	Pictures
Floor coverings	Radios, TVs, and VCRs
Flowers	Shoes
Gifts	Sporting goods
Greeting cards	Variety stores
Groceries	Women's clothing
Hardware	Women's accessories

Fig. 1-1. Small Retail Businesses.

Targeting the market

Before launching a business you must determine if a market exists and assess its size and growth potential. If a market does not exist, you must ascertain whether you can create a customer demand.

To target the market means to pinpoint your customers—who they are, where they are located, and what advertising media will reach them.

You must aim at the population segment with the best potential for building up a clientele. Aiming at everybody hits nobody. Even large department stores have discovered they cannot afford to be all things to all people. They have eliminated slow-selling clothing sizes and departments such as notions, fabrics, and needlecraft.

Targeting focuses efforts and establishes realistic, achievable objectives. It helps differentiate one store from its competitors and develop the store's unique market niche.

You must analyze the specific marketplace you are considering. Your choice may be geographic—the best neighborhood location in the largest city in the state. Or your business may be the kind that attracts customers no matter where the store is located—in a quiet, low-traffic area or a second floor walk-up shop.

Outline a profile of your customers, including their purchasing patterns in terms of size, price, style, and shopping hours. Ascertain potential buyers whom you may be able to attract with a carefully planned sales strategy. Pinpoint customer needs that seemingly are not fulfilled by competitors.

Competitors consist of every business after the same customers. Do not be afraid of competition; be aware but not wary. Competition is good for business—it creates customers by creating desires. Competitors' advertising helps you, as does their traffic. Shoppers like variety and choice, which your competitors provide.

In evaluating your ability to meet competition, you might start out by evaluating the competing stores' strengths and weaknesses, and what you plan to do better or differently. Make sure your store's merchandise is needed. Shopping trends have indicated that even the largest department stores need at least one neighboring department store.

Determining sales strategy

Sales strategy includes having the right product, the right price, the right sales personnel. It also includes sales promotion. When the image of the business has been defined and the price range and particular customers pinpointed, the merchant is ready to plan how to convince potential customers they should shop in his store.

Advertising is an expenditure for media publicity—newspapers, magazines, broadcasting, and billboards. Sales promotion may include direct mail, free handouts such as calendars, and redeemable coupons.

The market potential

Market research not only defines the market, it also indicates market potential. You may do your own research based upon federal reports, trade journals, the local chamber of commerce, the public library, telephone and mail and traffic surveys. The U.S. Department of Commerce via its Bureau of Census has issued a number of publications that present statistical data relating to the customer market. Your best resources are those that apply to your own locality, and their counsel is usually free—newspapers, magazines, television and radio studios, your wholesalers and manufacturers: they know the market potential.

Or you may use the services of a marketing research consulting firm. But be selective, and don't jump too quickly at bargain fees. Instead of asking if you can afford to obtain the services of professional marketing advisors, you should perhaps ask yourself if you can afford not to. In either event, whether doing your own research or using a professional consultant to whom you have defined your objectives, you must know your anticipated marketplace and customers, and the established competition in the area of your choice. A traffic count must produce as exact a set of figures as possible regarding the entire spectrum of market potential.

Naming the store

The name of the store sets its character—the image you wish to convey. It identifies you as the purveyor of a certain type of merchandise. The safest name is your own—no one can question its use. Should you choose to use another name, obviously it should not be one already in use. Acronyms often lead to disputes and even lawsuits. Many states require that such names be registered: this identifies the responsible person.

A franchise store usually carries the franchise name. When you buy a business an advantage may be that the buying terms include the privilege of retaining the name.

Look to the future in choosing the name, and visualize it on letterheads and in your advertising. The logo, the graphic symbol, becomes an important tool of recognition. An identifiable, unique logo conveys individuality. It should be informative as well as attractive. The information it gives may be words, pictures, or just an impression.

Licenses, permits, and registrations

Most small businesses require only city or county business licenses. They are obtainable at city or county offices. At the time of applying for such license you will be told if you must have a special permit for state or federal business operation. Check also with your state's department of commerce to see if you need such permits.

When you apply for the local license, you will also be told if you must have a special permit for operations that are considered hazardous.

A business must conform to zoning, building codes, and other regulations set by local health, fire, and police departments. There may be regulated setbacks of buildings from sidewalks, square-footage requirements, sign restrictions, and parking laws. Some kinds of businesses require special permits, and licensing for some occupations requires standards of professionalism, for example, pharmacies. The Interstate Commerce Commission has regulations relating to businesses involving meat products and drugs. If in doubt about your own store category, contact the Department of Commerce.

An employer's identification number is required on all employment tax returns. You obtain it by filing Form SS4 with your regional Internal Revenue Service (IRS) Center.

The Uniform Commercial Code governs basic types of daily business transactions. A copy is available from public libraries and bookstores. Every business owner should study it.

Your state may require registration of a fictitious name—a name other than yours or that of your partner or corporation. Contact the appropriate government agency to know what the requirements are. There may be a small registration fee, a requirement that you publish the trade name in a general-circulation newspaper in your store's area, and the filing of an affidavit in the county clerk's office confirming such publication. Sometimes the local newspaper will handle all of this for you.

If you have the traits of entrepreneurship and a store that will fill the needs of your targeted market, you're ready to roll.

2

Start-up alternatives

THE ALTERNATIVES IN GOING INTO BUSINESS ARE TO OPEN YOUR OWN STORE, TO buy an existing store, or to buy a franchise store. However you begin, the basic operation and economics are the same. All else being equal, it is practical to choose the one with the highest rate of return on your invested capital and time.

Starting from scratch

Opening a new business is the most difficult way of beginning, especially if you don't have any experience. You have to provide the capital and build a clientele, and you have expenses of starting and of early months of operation—in other words, high cost with little offsetting income. But there are advantages—you make a clean start, without business debts, in the location of your choice. And there is the satisfaction that with hard work and careful planning, with you as the innovator and planner, you can succeed.

Buying a business

There are advantages in buying an existing business. The risks are less, start-up time is eliminated, and hopefully you will have the same customers, the same suppliers, and the same volume of sales. Financial figures are available as the basis for accurate estimates of future sales and operating costs, and for seasonal buying of merchandise. You may benefit from the advice and experience of the owner, should she be willing to stay on for a short time. It's easier to establish credit with suppliers than when you start from scratch. You may be able to arrange financing with the seller, which is usually easier than bank financing. The owner may be willing to sell the business on contract, with an interest rate lower than the prevailing rate. You might even be able to acquire the store at a bargain price if the owner is eager to sell.

A disadvantage of buying an existing business might be that you inherit bad will as well as good will. It's important to know the store's reputation with its suppliers and its customers.

Another problem when buying an existing business is finding just the right one, in the right location, at the right price, at the right time.

Businesses for sale are listed in newspaper classified ads under "business opportunities," in trade journals and other publications in the public library, and in the Thursday edition of the *Wall Street Journal*. Or ask real estate agents or your bank. You might even pick out a shop you like and courageously approach the owner about buying it, or you might have someone do it for you.

Be realistic in your selection

Don't let your enthusiasm blind you to facts. Be realistic about the advantages and disadvantages of a store you consider buying. Find out why the owner wants to sell. His reasons may be good and legitimate. Perhaps he wishes to retire; perhaps his health demands it. But be wary of buying a store that is less than five years old.

What was the store's past performance? How many other owners were there, and why did they sell? What makes you think you will be successful if they were not?

Location is of prime importance. Does the city or section of the city suit your plans? Is the neighborhood going up or down? Will the traffic route change? Is the city planning highway construction that will affect your store?

What is the competition in the area? For example, a variety store's competition will be not only other variety stores but also hardware, drug, and fabric stores.

Are the store employees satisfactory, and will they stay on under new management? A hardware store found itself with no staff when it opened on Monday morning under new management. The buyer, with no hardware experience, had expected the manager and salespeople to guide her through a learning period.

Do you have to hire several people to replace the owner, who had done all of the work herself—bookkeeping, selling, cleaning?

How much is the business worth?

The business must be worth the asking price. The asking price is usually the net worth of the inventory and the equipment, minus the liabilities (the bills owed by the seller that the buyer is willing to assume). Good will is an added amount based upon the consistent profitability of the business—its earning power. The earning power is the true test of the value of the store. Good will may not be an acceptable consideration when buying a high-risk business, such as a gasoline station or other such highly competitive businesses.

Inventory and equipment

The liquidation value of the inventory and equipment is a negotiating figure. The appraisal must be accurate. An impartial person should do the appraisal if there is any question, out of fairness to both seller and buyer. In taking inventory of the stock and in determining its value, the average retail markup is deducted from the retail price, to which estimated freight cost may or may not be added. In determining the resulting value, deductions should be made relating to the merchandise age, condition, and salability. Obsolescence is a major consideration in drugstores, cosmetic stores, food markets. In fashion shops such as ladies' boutiques, fashion merchandise of the previous season, or even into the current season, is almost worthless. This applies to lingerie, shoes, and outerwear. It is particularly true in preteen and teen clothing stores for both boys and girls: fads and fancies travel fast in and out of the market. Another merchandise consideration is whether the store is overstocked.

Some of the equipment and fixtures may not be usable or necessary. Equipment attached to the building belongs to the building owner. In estimating sale value of equipment and fixtures, replacement value is a poor basis; book value (original cost less depreciation) is a sounder basis.

Negotiating the purchase price

The seller usually sets an asking price of about fifteen to twenty percent above the price he hopes to get. The buyer in his offer also leaves room for negotiation. If the business is offered at less than the book value, either the owner is naive or he knows something he has not divulged.

As the buyer, you must determine whether you can afford the store, taking into consideration how much you will need for the purchase price or down payment, and how much money you will have left to conduct the business and buy the next season's merchandise.

You should also consider how long it will take to pay for the business, and your percentage return on your investment. What salary did the owner draw, and what was the net earning in addition to the owner's salary? Will the anticipated cash flow be sufficient to maintain your standard of living?

Now that you know what it will cost to buy this store, how does it compare in cost with a business you could start yourself? Is it still to your advantage to buy a ready-made business?

If you are buying the business on contract, make an offer of the lowest down payment you think will be accepted. Set the lowest interest rate possible, with payments amortized over five or ten years. Try to have the seller stay on for a month or so, perhaps on a schedule of four hours a week. This gives you an opportunity to learn as much as possible about operation of the business and customers seeing the former owner with you will help smooth management turnover. In addition, require a customer list from the seller.

Now you'll need a lawyer

If you decide to go ahead, you will need an attorney to check the local bulk sales, zoning, and grandfather regulations, and the lease.

Bulk sales laws are designed to protect creditors of the seller of the business. There can be no secret sale of a business or its stock before creditors can take legal action to collect. These laws requires listing the creditors, their addresses, and amounts of indebtedness. The grandfather clause gives special permission to businesses in zoned areas to remain in business; this permission may not be transferable. The lease should be checked very carefully as to its transferability and renewability upon sale of the business.

When you buy a store from a merchant who is in a leased location, you and the seller may be entering into a landlord-and-tenant relationship for the duration of the lease. When the lease held by the seller of the business contains no restrictions, he can assign or sublease. The sublessee is responsible only to the original tenant for covenants of the sublease and not to the property owner. An assignment of a lease is an extension of the original lease, and transfers the tenant's interest to the buyer of the store. The assigned tenant, the new owner of the business, becomes obligated to the landlord under all of the lease covenants. When the seller is forbidden to sublet, a sublease is revocable by the landlord.

Mary Green was negotiating to buy a candy store, which was in a prime traffic location. It was in a rented storeroom. Her attorney, while examining the seller's lease, discovered that he had no authority to sublease or transfer the building to anyone else. The building owner had already negotiated to lease the premises to another owner when the present lease expired in three months. Had Mary Green bought the business, she would have had to find a new location six months later. The negotiated price had taken into consideration that she would not have had any advertising expenses because of the high-traffic location.

That was the fate of John Arnold. He had bought a chain of four florist shops. Six months later he found that he had paid for four stores but was the owner of only three. The "flagship" store, the one making the most profit and in a midtown location, had to go out of business because the owner would not renew the lease, and there was no other available location in the area.

Buying a franchise

When you buy a franchise store you buy a prepackaged business that operates under a contract with the parent organization. It is conducted as though it were part of a large corporation, with standardized products, equipment, and methods. An annual directory of franchising organizations is available from New York Pilot Industries.

Advantages

An advantage of a franchise business is that with limited experience you can become a merchant. The parent company has a stake in your successful operation. It will provide management assistance and business training for manager and staff. The difficulty in establishing credit rating by a newcomer in business may also be reduced. Benefits usually include start-up assistance such as help in site selection and setting up an accounting system. Merchandise is available from a central source. A recognized name, trademark, and national advertising shorten the start-up time in establishing a store image. Sometimes there is financial assistance, and help in layout and display design. The chance of failure is reduced because of the franchised products' reputation.

A good franchise is profitable and effective. However, there are good franchises and bad franchises; and the good ones are fewer, are seldom advertised for sale, and have long waiting lists for purchase.

Disadvantages

When considering affiliating with a franchise organization, investigate it carefully. The disadvantage of bad franchise companies is that their profits come not from operating the stores, but from selling them. They have been known to use high-pressure sales tactics and to make inflated promises. Be suspicious of a hard sell and evasion of your questions. When considering buying a franchise store, make sure that it has benefits over those of starting your own business. Compare its cost to that of starting your own store.

A disadvantage of operating a franchise store is that you will feel less like the boss. You may have to sell all of their products, even those not salable within your territory. Someone else will set the price, tell you how to do things, and require many written reports. You will share the franchise faults. And should you want to, you cannot just close or sell the store.

The parent organization

Even when you are considering buying a franchise store from another franchise store owner, get full details about the parent organization—when it was established, its history, profitability, and assets. Beware of a new organization, and of one with the reputation of foreclosing on an owner unable to make payments because they were based on unrealistic sales.

For a number of years, Helen Kane was an employee of a franchise cosmetic shop located on the third floor of an office building. She contracted to buy the shop from its owners, and the lease was transferred to her. She had confidence in her new role as owner, and knowing the customers, moved easily from employee to owner. A year later, the parent company sold a franchise to a store which would locate in ground floor space three blocks from Kane's store; there was promise of considerable pedestrian traffic for the competitive store.

Based upon Kane's experience, if you're considering franchise ownership, it's advisable to investigate the franchise parent company's policy regarding selling a franchise to more than one owner in a given area.

Talk to other franchise store owners of the organization you are considering. You are buying a name which may or may not carry weight with customers. If the franchise uses the name of a famous person, realize that personality prestige is perishable. A name may be important to the public today and not tomorrow.

If the products are imports, look for professional research regarding government decisions on tariff, import quotas, political climate, and value of foreign money. Overseas shipping reliability is of major concern to the business selling imports. Consider marine insurance, which covers land, water, and air transportation.

Centralized buying may be advantageous. Otherwise, you may not be able to get the stock. But make sure the franchiser is not tying you into contracts for purchases and services that could be bought on more advantageous terms elsewhere. Buying some items closer to home may make considerable difference in transportation costs and immediacy in restocking shelves. Some of the services that the franchiser wishes to sell you may not be advantageous.

The contract

Read the franchise contract carefully, and have your lawyer read it and advise you. Determine whether it is transferable should you ever want to sell the store. Know what the franchiser will provide in the way of initial and continuing assistance and services. All verbal agreements must be part of the written contract. Necessary contents of a contract to buy appear in Fig. 2-1.

When you consider buying the store not directly from the parent organization but from a store owner, examine its financial reports carefully—original cost, present book value, net profit. Some businesses keep two sets of books, one for

Complete description of all assets

Liabilities you will assume

Statement that all liabilities not listed will be the obligation of the seller

Tax obligations

Insurance obligations

Details of the sale, including all verbal agreements

Seller's warranty to protect buyer against inaccurate statements

Exact date seller will take possession

Who will pay legal fees

Agreement of seller not to compete

Exact purchase price

Method of payment

Time, place and procedure for closing

Fig. 2-1. Necessary Contents of Contract to Buy.

operational and the other for tax purposes; ask to see both of them. Examine the income tax reports for the past five years. Know the condition of the property, inventory, and equipment. Be aware of the competition in the area.

I had a satisfactory relationship with the parent organization of my franchised variety store. The monthly service of a company representative who took or reviewed the inventory of the countless number of items in the many departments simplified buying and kept me abreast of new and popular merchandise. However, I retained the right to buy additional merchandise from other suppliers, particularly local ones from whom I could buy in small quantities and restock as needed. I was my own bookkeeper, rather than using their system. I saved having to pay a fee for the service and also retained confidentiality.

Eventually I sold the store to a man who lacked variety store experience and needed all the help he could get. Despite my caution, he contracted with the parent organization for all of their services. Alas, his cash flow could not keep up with the fees he was paying.

Have your lawyer advise you of any relevant state and federal protective laws, franchise disclosure laws, and Federal Trade Commission (FTC) regulations. Additional information is available from the Washington, District of Columbia, office of the FTC, particularly a consumer bulletin entitled *Advice for Persons Who are Considering an Investment in a Franchise Business.*

3

Choosing the right location

BEFORE YOU DECIDE ON A BUSINESS SITE YOU MUST KNOW THE MARKET YOU plan to serve. You must also know the volume of business you may expect—income determines affordability. In other words, the location must be convenient for your customers; it must be affordable by your business.

Start out with a description of the ideal location and building as your goal. Then as you search, be realistic in modifying this description, staying as close to it as possible, keeping in mind your particular customers and sales potential. And when you ask yourself whether you can afford the particular location, remember that every additional rental dollar must generate additional sales volume.

Some facts to consider in choosing a location are itemized in Fig. 3-1.

Facts about commercial areas

Commercial or trade areas are those whose stores are in clusters —midtown or loop sections, shopping malls, neighborhood store clusters, heavily trafficked highways. The advantage of these areas is that they are trafficked and thus provide pedestrian drop-ins. Your store derives the benefit of customers and the other stores' advertising.

In small store clusters and in outlying areas there is less pedestrian traffic, but rent is lower. These areas are suitable for automobile agencies, automobile supply stores, hardware stores, and lumberyards.

Disadvantages for small stores in commercial areas include competition of big stores, high rent, parking meters. In "loop" sections, and in some neighborhood

The economic base

Retail sales per square foot

Industries that have closed lately

Industries scheduled to open

Number of empty store rooms

Number of failures in your kind of business

Street traffic in the daytime

Street traffic in the evening

Location of public transportation

Location of public parking

Condition of street lighting

Condition of parking lot lighting

Condition of sidewalks and highways

Regulations regarding your kind of business

Crime rate

Customers

What is the employment rate?

Where do residents work?

Is major shopping done in other cities or areas?

Competition

Who are they? the nearest? the biggest?

Are they prospering?

Do they have frequent markdown sales?

Are there other stores that sell your product? Why not?

Other considerations

Volume of traffic

Space for future expansion

Parking facilities

Quality of life for owner-manager and family

Availability of potential employees

Fig. 3-1. The Location: Facts to Consider.

strip sections, pedestrian traffic ceases at nightfall, and there may not be Sunday business hours.

Traffic flow is only one measurement for selecting a location. Availability is also a factor. Customers will go to malls and midtown business areas when shopping for clothing and appliances because they like to do comparative shopping. They will drive a greater distance to buy furniture and major appliances. Distance is no deterrent to reaching department stores and discount houses because of their prices, products, and management. Such stores build their own traffic flow.

There are favorable and less favorable locations, whether in malls or other shopping areas, and often one side of the street or mall corridor is better than another. For stores on city streets or highways, the "going home" side is preferred to the "going to work" side, and the shady side is preferred to the sunny side.

Importance of accessibility

Pedestrian traffic and unrestricted parking time are particularly conducive to customers browsing variety, book, greeting card, apparel, and toy stores. Consider the matter of parking meters where there is sufficient parking space in the vicinity: are they restrictive because of time limitations and cost, or do they keep traffic moving by making parking space available more frequently than on unmetered streets?

In large cities, public transportation is the usual mode of travel, so parking lots are of less importance. But public transportation is always important to nondrivers—senior adults, the handicapped, and children; therefore, it's important to businesses in the area.

Automobile traffic, particularly on highways, may impede shopping; it may be so fast that cars cannot stop in front of the store, or that pedestrians on the other side cannot safely cross the street.

Tom Heatherington owned an attractive building on a well-traveled street. He could not understand why he had difficulty keeping tenants. When another tenant moved out after one year, Heatherington opened a china and crockery store in that location. The customers he sought did not respond to newspaper or radio advertising, cut-price sales, coupons, even a large, attractive sign on the building. Finally, he realized that the heavy traffic was a hindrance, not a help. Speeding cars discouraged motorists from turning into his parking lot. Pedestrians on the other side of the street hesitated about crossing over. He found a health spa tenant who did not need drop-in customers. He moved his china and crockery store to a pedestrian-trafficked strip and did well. So did the health spa.

How shopping malls work

Shopping malls vary in size and type. Super regional shopping centers or malls are comparable to central business districts of cities. They often have two or three major department stores as main tenants, and their scope of merchandise is similar to that in a business district. A smaller mall may have one department store that also offers a wide variety of merchandise as its main tenant.

The rent in malls is usually a base amount plus a percentage of gross sales. There are regulations such as those regarding shopping hours.

When you rent a "shell" in the mall you get four walls, a roof, and a dirt floor; you provide the electrical and plumbing fixtures and interior walls. A "half shell" means you get doors, wallboard, concrete floors; you may or may not get heat and plumbing. "Key" or "turnkey" means you get a finished space ready to decorate. "Will divide to suit" means the landlord pays for structural changes, and the tenant provides decorating inside and out.

The value of the particular shopping center to your kind of business should carry weight in making a decision. It's advisable to study the types of business in the area, whether mall or store cluster, to identify customer characteristics. It may be a center that specializes in discount stores. It may be a good location for a pet shop but not a jewelry store. A ladies' boutique would not be well served by a neighboring meat market, or a seed store by a location in which frequent shoppers are apartment dwellers.

Consider with caution downtown pedestrian malls closed to vehicular traffic. Shoppers are less interested in brick sidewalks, flowers, and trees than in the convenience of being able to park close by. "Most of them have been horrible failures," said Kenneth Stone, an Iowa State University economics professor. "They were built as a response to big shopping malls, a way to get people back downtown. Unless a city has a special situation, it is likely to be in trouble. Unless traffic patterns and parking are taken into account, they cannot be successful."

Cities that have spent millions of dollars installing such pedestrian malls and skywalks are considering spending additional large amounts of money to restore street-level customer traffic.

Researching the area

Marketing research organizations provide expertise for exploring business areas. Such information is available also from the local chamber of commerce, industrial commissions, trade sources, bankers, and representatives of your merchandise suppliers. They might have information about types of businesses which the town lacks, such as supermarkets or pharmacies. City planning departments and engineering offices have data about traffic patterns and plans for highways.

But do your own study as well. In analyzing traffic flow to determine if there are enough pedestrians to support your business, look for packages, as well as people. They may be lookers, not buyers, in the area for reasons other than shopping.

Investigate the area on foot; talk to property owners. Know about plans for urban development, zoning, new industries. Know the history of the region. Has there been flooding and could it happen again? Have toxic fumes from a nearby factory been a source of concern for residents? Will access to the store be cut off for any length of time because of work on the pavement?

Zoning and other government regulations

In existing shopping centers, zoning is not a problem unless it applies to businesses which by their nature carry restrictions—liquor stores, fast food shops, dance halls.

In restricted areas, Grandfather clauses protect certain existing businesses because they were in that location before the law was adopted; this privilege may not be inherited by new owners of the businesses.

Restrictions considered unreasonable by a business owner can be appealed to designated officials.

There are strict regulations—city, state, federal—regarding health, safety, and facilities for the handicapped. There are also building code requirements for setbacks at the front, side, and rear of buildings, as well as regarding building heights and parking space.

Moving to a new city

If you are opening your store in a city other than the one in which you now live, all circumstances affecting the location must be considered. Choose a city where there is more than one payroll industry so there is diversification of income sources. Otherwise, severe economic loss to the entire community is suffered with the payroll loss when the one industry closes.

Jacobsons was a workingman's clothing store. When the Rock Island Railroad closed its shops and the cement plants moved away, Jacobsons survived by converting into an apparel store for the entire family.

Consider your family's welfare, including health considerations such as allergies and proximity of good schools and churches. Tour the residential area and evaluate residents by their homes and cars. Speak to the residents and the chief officer of the Small Business Association. Count people in the business section during various times of the day. Are they carrying parcels? Study license plates to find out where they live. Study statistics regarding population, income, and sales: are they larger or smaller than five years ago?

Starting a cottage industry

The advantages of working out of your home are that there is savings in rent, commuting, child care, overhead, start-up, and certain taxes.

The disadvantages include no family life privacy and a less professional image. Suppliers may refuse credit or delivery in a noncommercial area. A woman with household tasks is prone to give less time to business.

There are ways to overcome the disadvantages. Privacy is preserved by setting up definite working hours, and separating private life from business life. Using a post office box address gives formality for prestige purposes with suppliers. In addition, an answering machine or service, separate telephone lines, and telephones with hold buttons and multiple lines that distinguish between business and private telephone usage are other ways of separating family from business activities.

Watch out for zoning restrictions

It usually is illegal to have a business in a residential area without zoning board approval. Regulations state what businesses can and cannot be carried on in the home, thus safeguarding the residential area. Where store signs are permitted, there is limitation on their size. Some zoning laws for residential areas permit businesses only on corners of the blocks.

Established businesses in the area may be protected by a grandfather clause that does not apply to new businesses or takeover by a new tenant. Most residential zoning allows a business if it is incidental to the use of the home, but forbids outside signs and merchandise displays. Some zoning permits home businesses if most of what is sold is made in the home, and no unusual amount of traffic is generated.

You can apply for zoning variance, and if taken to court for having a business in a restricted area, you can claim that the business will not produce noise, fumes, or disorder; that there will be a private garbage-disposal arrangement, and no increased need for services relating to sewers; that the business will not be open to the public; and that the number of customers will be small, and their parking will not interfere with neighboring parking needs.

Tax advantages of retailing at home

To be eligible for IRS acceptance—in other words, to be able to take tax deductions for operating in your home—there must be a definite area of the house devoted to the business.

If the business takes up ten percent of the floor space of the house, you can deduct ten percent of fuel, utilities, depreciation, and other costs of running the house. You can deduct rent, but you cannot deduct mortgage or real estate taxes because they are fully deductible whether or not you have a home business or office. The maximum permissible deduction is the business gross income minus ten percent of mortgage interest and taxes. If there is more than one business location, the maximum deduction is the gross income attributable to that location, less the relevant percentage of interest and taxes. In such instances, it is advisable to get exact information from the IRS.

In a partnership, each partner can take home business deductions if her home satisfies the test either as the business or the business office.

In the case of a children's bookstore, the book business was in May's home, and the office work was done in Sue's home; both were entitled to a tax deduction. Whether sole proprietorship, partnership, or Subchapter S corporation (described in Chapter 17), the expense of operating a business or its offices in a home is deductible if at least one of the following is true:

1. It is the principal place of business.

2. Clients and customers come there in the ordinary course of business.

3. The structure belongs to, but is separate from, the house and is used in connection with the business.

4. The house is the only fixed location for the business, and the home office is used regularly to store business inventory.

If yours is a corporation that has not elected Subchapter S, you can collect rent for the business or its office from the corporation; you get a business deduction for the full amount of rent, even if the rent is higher than the office's proportionate share of house expenses. The rent you receive from the corporation is ordinary income and is so reported on Schedule 1040. The home office must be an identifiable area but need not be a separate room.

For precise information on the law governing home industries, get the latest edition of IRS Publication 587, *Business Uses of Your Home,* and also Internal Revenue Code 280A.

4

The building

HAVING DECIDED ON THE BEST LOCATION FOR YOUR STORE, YOU ARE READY TO
consider the building in that area. Whether you rent or buy property, considerations are the same as to size of building or room, its physical condition, and suitability for your needs.

Some building characteristics and features to consider are listed in Fig. 4-1.
Yours may be a business which has some specific requirements, such as

delivery access

loading dock

ramp

rear exit

entry availability before or after usual store hours

special plumbing or electrical requirements

conformity to certain safety and health regulations, any or all of which must
be taken into consideration.

To buy or to rent

In determining whether to rent or buy a location, take into consideration tax and
maintenance costs, and whether your business will be stable enough at the very
beginning of your operation to carry a mortgage. To evaluate purchasing the property, you also must consider how it will be financed, payment terms, and amount
of the down payment.

The building must:

Be structurally sound and meet certificate of occupancy requirements;

Comply with zoning and fire laws, and city regulations relating to front entrance canopies, awnings, and signs;

Be large enough to meet the requirements of the business;

Have space for expansion.

Features to consider:

1. Front entrance steps are a disadvantage for the handicapped, the elderly, and those with baby carriages.

2. Glass doors permit a view of the interior from the street, an advantage after closing hours.

3. Show windows create an appetite for the merchandise and give an image of the store, but they need constant cleaning and redecoration, take up selling space, and in a crime area invite break-in.

4. Retail store should estimate 80 percent of floor space for selling; 20 percent for workroom, storage, office, dressing rooms, rest rooms.

5. L-shaped or long and narrow rooms may require additional sales staff.

6. Careful check should be made of heating and air conditioning equipment, and of electrical outlets and telephone jacks.

Fig. 4-1. The Store Building.

George and Mary Cole applied to the SBA for a loan to buy a business and the building in which it was located. They were turned down. They went back to the seller, who agreed to lease them the building for two years, with option to buy at the end of that period. Again they applied to SBA for a start-up loan to buy only the business. They received the loan.

You remain more flexible when you rent. As the business grows you can move to a bigger place. Meanwhile, your rent is tax deductible as a current business expense. As in the case of George and Mary Cole, it is more difficult to get a bank or SBA loan to cover both the start-up of a business and the purchase of a building.

Getting the best purchase price or rent

To estimate a reasonable purchase price or rent, talk to real estate agents or your banker. If you are considering buying the building, have an appraiser confirm its value. A good location can bring you profit; a bad site can result in disaster. You determine the amount of rent you can afford by estimating your net business income.

Don't choose a place just because the rent or purchase price is low. The price may reflect the desirability of the location. And so in looking for an answer to the question, "Can I afford this place?" keep in mind that a good traffic location decreases advertising costs. Visibility is a major asset. Advertising costs are the expenses of using artificial means to create visibility. According to an SBA manual, "Rent is the combination of space and advertising." In other words, the better the site, the less you may need to spend on advertising.

It is usual for the base rent to be modified by an escalator clause—which means that rent is raised as the building owner's costs go up; it is a reflection, usually, of an increase in property tax. Learn if there are other fees payable by the tenant to the landlord. The landlord may require a rental deposit. In some states this deposit must be in an interest-bearing account, the tenant remaining in full ownership.

If you choose to rent

If you decide to become a tenant, determine the following before signing the lease:

who pays for renovation and capital improvements

who pays for immediate and later repairs

who provides for such services as
    heat
    air conditioning
    janitor service
    trash pick-up
    sidewalk cleaning
    elevator service

who pays for fire and liability insurance

who is obligated to maintain insurance coverage before tenant occupancy.

The lease

Do not assume that the building is in good repair at the time of taking occupancy. Know whether you are leasing "as is," and if not, what repairs the owner will make before the lease starts. The tenant may be able to get a lesser rent by taking the storeroom with the proviso that he will do his own minor repairs, or that he may deduct the expense of repairs from the rent.

The tenant needs the owner's permission to alter the building; further, the tenant may be required to restore the building to its original condition when he moves. The lease should stipulate in what condition the tenant must leave the premises, or his original rent deposit could be in jeopardy.

Marjorie Trout, as a first-time entrepreneur, wanted to cover all bases in her new venture. Her business was a store that carried vintage clothing, and was best located in the "Old Town" of her city. She was able to get a long-term lease with privilege of subletting. She wanted to protect her established business should she later discover that she needed larger premises. She also wanted a way out should her business prove to be unprofitable, and not to be stuck with paying rent for the unexpired term.

Lease clauses are negotiable

If the lease says, "Maintain the premises in good repair," substitute "Take good care of the premises and fixtures."

There are laws to cover termination of the lease if the property is made untenable by fire or other damage. In some instances a provision in the lease may supersede the statute; your lawyer will advise you in this regard. In any event, delete from a lease the statement, "If the building is damaged by fire or other cause without fault or neglect of the tenant, tenant shall not claim compensation because of inconvenience caused by such fire."

If the building is under construction when the lease is signed, the tenant should require that the lease allow for rent rebate if the building is not ready for occupancy when scheduled. Delete from the lease, "Landlord shall not be liable for failure to give possession on said date."

Delete from the lease the following clauses:

"Additional financial obligations which may arise."

"Tenant agrees to obey all reasonable rules and regulations as the landlord may from time to time make or adopt."

". . . and any additional rent as the landlord may designate from time to time."

Part II

Charting a successful store operation

5

The role of the owner/manager

MANAGEMENT OF A LARGE BUSINESS IS IN THE HANDS OF A NUMBER OF PEOPLE, each with a special area function. The small business has the same number of area functions but all of them are handled by one person: you. Even if some areas of management are totally foreign to your education and experience, you must handle them until you are ready to delegate.

At the outset, finances may not be the only deterrent in engaging a staff. It is your store. You want everything to be done according to your plan. There is merit in going it alone. As you involve yourself in all areas of concern, you are learning every aspect of the business. You will make mistakes—but they are mistakes important to your learning process. When you are ready to delegate responsibilities, you will be a better boss because you have done every job yourself and will know how it should be done, time involved, and cost. You will have become a better all-around store executive.

The success of a business depends upon good management. Bad management spells failure. You detect bad management in insufficient sales, heavy operating expenses, uncollectible accounts, and inventory problems. There could be costly errors of omission—failure to create loyal customers, inadequate records, meager inventory control, inattention to a changing market, and growing neighborhood competition.

The many hats of the manager

Effective management requires:

1. planning
2. organizing
3. controlling
4. improving
5. decision-making policies

The manager as planner

Planning involves budgeting money, time, and resources. Resources include human resources, and you, at the outset, are the vital human resource who is bookkeeper, buyer, salesperson, advertising director, and most likely even maintenance personnel (another name for janitor). Add staff when it will contribute to profits and growth—when it will free you for more profitable activity.

The manager as organizer

Organizing involves activating all of the plans made for achieving the business goals. The manager's responsibilities encompass everything relating to money, staffing, merchandise methods, and not in that order: they are all top line objectives. He makes sure that all work is done and in accordance with planned objectives. The controlling goal is profit.

The manager as controller

Controlling entails constant evaluation of performance in every aspect. You set procedures not only for achieving goals but also for solving problems, which are bound to arise. Policy precedes procedure. Policy is established in order to avoid recurring problems; it determines the procedure, which is the method of operation—the blueprint. The procedures in writing can be called "the company policy."

The manager as improver

Hindsight is experience recalled—it becomes foresight for future planning. The good manager evaluates and corrects, improving the business operation and anticipating the future as he plans for growth and success.

If sales have dropped, what was wrong? Was it the merchandise? Overordering? Underordering? Insufficient advertising? Was there insufficient capital? Were expenses excessive? Good records will enable you to be objective in your analysis rather than defensive in your appraisal.

The manager as a member of the staff

As the manager, you must evaluate yourself. Stop trying to do everyone else's job. You may do the work of two people, but you are not two people. Organize your day. Learn to delegate. Plan not to be off the floor during heavy traffic time. Should you come into the store before opening time in order to do work, don't answer the telephone; keep that hour as uninterrupted time. Salesmen representing your suppliers arrive unannounced; save time for them.

The manager as employer

Human resources could be your most valuable asset if recognized as such; efficient help makes business grow. As an employer it's important that you select good staff members and train them for your particular business. Temporary help may be a money saver—you use these people when you need them—but unless you give them careful instruction they will not know your standards of operation. As your business grows, your staff will increase by necessity. At the very outset, with only one or two employees, set the pattern for your staff requirement, and the accompanying compensation expense. Salary may become your biggest expense.

The manager as decision and policymaker

The manager's responsibilities as the decision maker are to define the policies and set goals to be reached in step-by-step stages.

Delegating the store's operation

Being a store owner should continue to be an enjoyable and exciting experience. To maintain it as such, look for time release, not only to be able to function entirely as the manager of the establishment, but also time to "smell the roses." A small business usually needs only one full-time executive: you. However, you should seek help, to do the jobs you cannot do or should not be doing in order to make the best use of your own time.

You may be a pretty good bookkeeper yourself, but, not to be deskbound, you may wish to hire a bookkeeper, full- or part-time, or train an employee to follow routinely the pattern established by your certified public accountant (CPA).

You know you have salesmanship ability, and you appreciate the importance of personal contact with your customers, but to release yourself from being salesfloor bound, you hire a salesperson.

Jim Jeffrey, who owned a chain of ladies' sportswear stores, was having difficulty paying off an SBA loan. As a SCORE counselor I studied his operation, but I didn't have to go farther than his office door. He spent most of his time in the office, and his records were meticulous. On the salesfloor were two chic young ladies, engrossed in "being chic" rather than in helping potential customers become equally chic. And these young ladies were the ones who were actually "keeping the store."

The answer to Jim Jeffrey was, do your bookwork before or after store hours, and get out on the salesfloor and see what is going on out there.

To free yourself from as many routine functions as possible and have time to concentrate on managerial responsibilities, list all of your self-assigned tasks, and then determine which can be assigned to someone else.

Professional services

For smooth day-to-day operation, look to professional services before you open your store for business. Don't wait until you get into serious trouble before lining up a lawyer, a CPA, and a banker. Don't let pride stand in your way of telling these specialists in what areas you need advice. Tell them your plans so they may help you achieve your objectives.

Lawyer   You will need a lawyer. In this day of specialization, choose one who has had experience in working with small businesses. You go to him not to have him make your decisions, but to serve as your consultant and advisor. First arrange an interview, for which you should not be charged, and describe your operation. Don't look for a bargain, but know the lawyer's hourly rates for both office conferences and telephone calls. Require a detailed bill at the end of the month.

Certified public accountant   At first the entrepreneur may think he cannot afford to use the services of an accountant. However, an experienced accountant could be a money saver because of his expertise. He can set up a bookkeeping system geared to your specific business and show you how to keep the records current. He can show you how to interpret these figures as a business operational tool. If a business cannot afford this expenditure, perhaps the entrepreneur really cannot afford to go into business.

Local trade associations and business colleagues are excellent sources for recommending an accountant—one who operates independently or who is a member of an accounting firm that is small and has time for you and considers you an important client.

It is important that the accountant be one with whom you have good rapport and of whom you feel free to ask questions.

Expect him to give you an explanation of tax procedures and deductions. Inform him of your objectives, your method of operation, your management system as well as all financial data. His services should be tailored to meet the needs of your business. You should know what services to expect from him and how they relate to analysis of the health of your operation—because it is for you to make all business decisions, and not the CPA. However, his realistic approach could be a practical counterpoint to your enthusiasm.

Banker   Before selecting a banker as your advisor, select a bank, taking into consideration its services, location, and charges. Then choose the officer of the bank with whom you will want to work.

Where to go for help

The U.S. SBA is not only a source for business loans, it is also superior as a counseling source, free upon request via its affiliated agencies.

SCORE (Service Corps of Retired Executives), volunteers the services of retired experts in every area of business needs; it provides one-on-one counseling for as long as the merchant requests, and regularly schedules classes on going into business.

Small Business Development Centers (SBDC) operate mainly in conjunction with colleges and universities; the counselors are professors and businesspeople. The counselors are paid for their services by the government; the counseling to the client is free. It is a valuable service, not only to those who wish to go into business, but also to ongoing businesses that have particular problems or wish to expand.

SBA provides business analysis by college students under their instructor's supervision; an ongoing business may request this study of its operation. This too is free.

The owner of a fabric shop was highly critical of an SBA team's work: The analysis was that overhead was too high because the impressive location of the business was too large and too costly. "What do those school kids know?" was the owner's verdict. Two years later, on the verge of bankruptcy, she moved her business into much smaller quarters in a highly trafficked mall and dropped her dressmaking classes, which had required large classrooms. Today her business is flourishing.

SBA has a wealth of printed materials, free for the asking, all written for the small business owner and covering every area of entrepreneurship, especially the small retail store.

Throughout the country, seminars on the operation of small businesses are sponsored by SBA, SCORE, SBDC, chambers of commerce, the U.S. Department of Commerce, banks, universities, and other organizations.

Still more sources of help

Suppliers of merchandise are gold mines of information via their sales representatives.

You might also discover new ideas through discussion with business professionals at local meetings hosted by the chamber of commerce, business organizations, or merchants' associations.

Trade journals and other publications provide information and statistics of businesses similar to your own.

Professional counselors are listed in your telephone book; for reference, ask for the names of their clients.

6
Managing your personnel

FOR A SMALL STORE, PARTICULARLY AT THE VERY BEGINNING, A GOOD EMPLOYEE is one who can handle a variety of routine responsibilities. He is a boon to the overburdened manager.

Before hiring your first employee, determine the job requirements. Write out a job description that defines clearly and unmistakably all responsibilities and duties.

To find employees, consult newspaper classified ads, state employment services, local high schools and colleges. Or pay a fee to an employment agency, or put a sign in your store window.

Enthusiastic recommendations by well-meaning friends of applicants might not always serve your best interests. It is also well to avoid hiring friends or relatives. To hire a manager or a department head, when you reach that rung in your ladder of growth, you might look to trade journals or to your suppliers for recommendations. Look for employees who have experience and who are:

enthusiastic

willing to work hard

friendly

alert

intelligent

cooperative

flexible

neat in appearance

poised

able to communicate clearly

Five steps of hiring

As you begin the hiring process, keep in mind various laws protecting employees' rights. Simply stated, equal employment opportunity regulations make it illegal to discriminate against an applicant on the basis of race, religion, sex, national origin, or age.

The rights of qualified handicapped persons are protected by the Rehabilitation Act of 1973. Additional regulations mandated by the 1990 Americans with Disabilities Act are being phased in.

Workers' compensation laws protect employees in case of disabilities incurred on the job, including liability for related medical costs.

The Fair Labor Standards Act establishes a basic wage and hour law, provides overtime compensation for hours worked in excess of the standard number of hours in a work week, prohibits oppressive child labor employment, and protects females against discrimination in wages. Laws also prevent age discrimination in employment.

Step 1. The application

The application blank helps screen the applicant. It should include name, address, telephone number, education, job experience, character references, references from former employers. Standard forms are available from stationery stores. Keep in mind that the questions you ask verbally or in writing must be relevant to the job. Asking for a photograph or the following information is considered discriminatory:

marital status

birthplace

age

religion

membership in organizations

wife's maiden name

applicant's maiden name

relatives (After hiring it is permissible to get names of persons to notify in case of emergency.)

arrests (You can, however, ask about convictions.)

children

height and weight

possessions (car, house)

job of spouse, father, mother

Step 2. Screening the applicant

If possible, screen applicants before selecting them for interviews. This should be done when the applicant presents the filled-out application form. Screening is the process of eliminating unqualified applicants, a process of assessment in order to decide whom to reject.

Step 3. The first interview

Put the applicant at ease by having him do the talking first, but don't answer his questions until he has answered yours. Keep in mind that you are looking for long-time commitment. Explain the importance of the job. Point out that whereas the acknowledged advantages of working for big businesses are fringe benefits and possibly larger salaries, the compensations of a small business are pleasant working conditions, informality, less monotony because of the variety of roles, and training and opportunity for a better future and perhaps becoming a store owner.

Step 4. Reference checks

Check personally all references offered by job applicants. You can use a form letter and questionnaire, or you can check in person or by telephone. The telephone is quickest and most reliable. You can tell a lot from hesitancy in answering a question; you could follow up with diplomatic questions that might provide important answers.

Avoid references from relatives, neighbors, people in political positions, and church officials. The employee will select people whom he thinks will give him the best recommendations. If he doesn't give the name of a present or former employer, or if there is a decided gap in his employment history, he may have something he doesn't want to tell you.

Sometimes his former employer may be unfair in his evaluation due to a personality conflict or an unfortunate happening. On the other hand, he may not wish to jeopardize the employee's chance of finding a job. So it's important to use your own good judgment in evaluating what you have been told while checking references.

There are firms that specialize in investigating, but they usually are useful only when investigating a person being considered for a position of trust. The local credit bureau might provide you with an individual's entire background—education, employment, and other pertinent information. Check the current law, or have your lawyer do it, relating to fair credit reporting before using such an agency.

Usually the best source of reference is a former boss. Telephone him. End your questions with, Would you re-hire this person?

Step 5. The second interview

In this interview you relate information about the store and the specifics of the job.

Training: The key to increased sales

The initial training period of the new employee takes into account the trauma of the person who has never before had to handle a cash register, make change, fill out a variety of sales slips.

Don't overwhelm the new employee with a barrage of information, as I did when looking for an assistant manager of my department store—a position with a lot of responsibilities. I found a likely candidate, and on the first day on the job, from 9:00 A.M. until noon I explained the entire operation of the store—layout of merchandise, staff assignments, clearing cash registers at the end of the day, charge accounts, and on and on. He left at noon for lunch and didn't return—not even for his half-day's pay. I had to mail that to him, but I admitted the error of my ways and regretted that he was no longer interested in taking the position.

Neither should you understate the responsibilities of the position. In a retail store the salesperson must know that there is a first-thing-in-the morning routine of housekeeping and dusting, and a periodic inventory count. There may be a mid-morning coffee break, but absolutely no first-thing-in-the-morning breakfast break for employees. They must arrive ready to work. A recommended schedule for employee training appears in Fig. 6-1, and some staff do's and don'ts in Fig. 6-2.

Salesmanship

In the retail store, selling is everyone's business—the writer of the newspaper ad, the window trimmer, the person who happens to answer the telephone, the bookkeeper who is on the sales floor clearing the cash register when a customer asks about merchandise. Your customer judges your store by the one he usually meets—the salesperson or you—but he also comes in contact with others, whether he's paying a bill or inquiring about something he saw in the window.

Your strongest asset is your (and your employees') personal relationships with your customers. These relationships should be friendly and cordial, and you must train the entire staff to create that image.

If yours is a self-service discount or variety store, take a page from the book of supermarkets that in their advertising boast of "service with a smile, in every aisle." Even the stock clerk unpacking crates as he stocks the shelves or fills the fruit bins should be expected to answer questions if customers want to know the location of an item or how to select a melon.

The success of your store is in large measure in the hands of the salesperson. Your goal is to sell merchandise. Of all of the abilities that you look for when hiring a salesperson the top ability necessary to the success of your store is that he be able to sell merchandise. If you expect only honesty and courtesy you will be hiring glorified package wrappers, with no salesmanship. See Fig. 6-3 for a lesson in salesmanship.

Day one

Make him feel at home: He may be shy about asking you some questions, so assign a buddy for the first few days.

Introduce staff and the duties of each one.

History of the store

Policy of the store

Job description and work schedule

Store hours

Parking and transportation facilities

Use of business telephone

Rest periods

Pay periods

Vacations and holidays

Other benefits and rules

Day two

Merchandise and its location

Salesmanship—how to approach a customer

Daily housekeeping duties and care of merchandise

Day three

Cash register procedure

How to make change

How to write sales slips

Policy rechecks, credit cards, charge accounts

Merchandise returns and exchanges

Package and gift wrapping

Salesmanship

Day four

Selling on floor, with buddy nearby

Second week

Review of lessons of first week

How to take inventory of one department

Fig. 6-1. Schedule for Employee Training.

DO be enthusiastic about the merchandise and the store.

DO know the store services available to customers.

DON'T oversell, or act disgruntled if the customer does not buy.

DO refresh the stock between customers, and keep busy.

DON'T stand idly in the doorway or look out of the window.

DO cooperate with the rest of the staff.

DON'T point when customers ask the location of merchandise—lead them to it.

DON'T chitchat on the telephone while customers are waiting; customers in the store take priority over those on the telephone.

DO handle merchandise with respect—customers are exchanging good money for it.

DON'T keep a customer waiting—promise service shortly.

Periodic evaluation of sales staff

Are the salespeople losing sales?

Is their attitude one of being ready to help customers?

Do they stop whatever else they are doing to take care of customers?

Do they show they know the merchandise? store services?

Do they allow browsing time, but show readiness to help?

Fig. 6-2. Staff Dos and Don'ts.

Jack Edwards, salesperson in the men's department, is busy arranging a new shipment of shirts, when a customer enters his department. He immediately stops what he is doing.

Jack: Good morning, Mrs. Pearson. How may I help you this morning?

Mrs. Pearson: Oh, I'm just looking around today.

Jack returns to his work with the shirts on the counter, keeping an eye on Mrs. Pearson, should she appear to be interested in a particular item.

Jack: The shirts that you are looking at just came in today. The workmanship is superior. Here, let me show you what I mean. (He removes a plastic cover from a shirt.) Let me show you the double seams. Feel the quality of the fabric.

Mrs. Pearson: It is a beautiful shirt. It probably is expensive, more than I want to pay.

Jack: No, the quality is there, but you aren't taxed for that. This shirt is $24.95.

Mrs. Pearson: Do you have it in white, size 16?

Fig. 6-3. A Lesson in Salesmanship.

Jack: Yes, we do, because the shirts just today came in. You have made an excellent choice. The ties on this rack are new as well. Aren't they beautiful?

Mrs. Pearson: Yes, especially this blue one. I'll take it to go with the shirt.

Jack writes up the sales slip and rings up the sale.

Jack: Is this going to be a gift? I'll be glad to gift wrap it for you, Mrs. Pearson.

Mrs. Pearson: I would appreciate that.

Jack wraps the shirt, hands it to Mrs. Pearson.

Jack: Thank you; it has been a pleasure, as usual, waiting on you.

He walks Mrs. Pearson to the entry.

Jack's demonstration of salesmanship

1. He greeted Mrs. Pearson by name.
2. He stopped what he was doing in order to help her.
3. He asked, "How may I help you?" not, "May I help you?"
4. He did not stalk her as she browsed.
5. He was alert to the moment she was interested in buying.
6. He pointed out particular qualities of the shirt.
7. He invited tactile as well as visual examination.
8. He encouraged another purchase without asking, "Is there anything else?"
9. He handled the shirt and tie with loving care.
10. He suggested another service of the store—free gift wrapping.
11. He thanked her for making the purchase.
12. He "walked her to the door" as he would a guest in his home.

Fig. 6-3. Continued.

The employer as motivator

The manager as employer must be a motivator. Unmotivated employees can kill an otherwise successful business. Salary is not enough motivation. You want employees who work with enthusiasm. An executive of a large international company said that management is nothing more than motivating people, and the only way to motivate people is to communicate with them.

As a boss, know how to demonstrate and to explain clearly, carefully, and patiently. Give credit; when you give a raise, increase responsibilities. Reward employees for accomplishments, and at the same time motivate them to do even better. Inculcate the desire to make money for the store, but always exemplifying the store policy of integrity. As the boss you must be ready to encourage, advise, suggest, and let employees know you appreciate their value to the business.

Your relationship with your employees

Be concerned about your employees, and train supervisors, if you have them, to be concerned about your employees. An employee's loyalty results from his confidence that you respect him, that you will listen when he comes to you with suggestions or problems. Show your interest in his ideas. Treat him as an individual; show your interest in him. Be fair and don't show favoritism. Encourage opportunities for advancement by advancing staff from within whenever possible. Compliment on specifics. Express appreciation publicly; offer criticism privately and in the form of suggestions. Should you find it necessary to reprimand, end with a statement of encouragement.

Be tolerant. Andrew Carnegie's philosophy was, "You can make as many mistakes as you like, but don't make the same mistake twice."

The employer-employee relationship is self serving. You may have prima donnas who are good producers: keep them happy.

The owner of a chain of shoe stores came to me with the problem that one of his store managers was his top producer, but he failed to have his inventory records ready by noon on Mondays because he allowed himself to be interrupted by customers who would insist that he wait on them. My advice to him was to appoint another member of the staff to do the shoe counting on Monday mornings.

Encourage responsibility and ingenuity of employees, but without losing control of the situation yourself. Do not do what I did, which evidently was interpreted as freedom to act by a new young man in my shoe department on his very first day. When I got back to the store after lunch, he had rearranged not only the chairs but the stock of the whole shoe department. It took us two days to get the merchandise back to where we could find anything, my penalty for taking a two hour lunch break.

Salaries

Salaries should be fair and just; they depend upon the bracket of employment. Establish a salary level for each type of job—maintenance, bookkeeping, selling, managing, and buying. Determine the minimum and maximum.

Some businesses pay salary plus commission; for example, men's clothing, floor coverings. Some businesses may pay commission only; for example, automobiles, furniture. In some selling positions, salary depends upon accumulated amount of monthly sales—base pay plus an "award for ability"—for example, for sales up to $2,500, up to $4,000, or up to $6,000. In such a system, employee sales records are reviewed every six months.

Salaries may be figured hourly, weekly, semi-monthly, or monthly.

Fringe benefits

Even the smallest store can offer fringe benefits. Vacation with pay could consist of: three days for employment of six months, one week for one year's employment, two weeks for those who have worked for two to three years, and three weeks for those who have worked longer than that.

Enumerate to the employee the paid holidays. Retail stores often are open on holidays. Salaries may be the regular amount, or overtime pay equivalent to $1\frac{1}{2}$ or double the regular amount.

Sick days may be an allowance of up to three days for each six months of employment, and limited to a week sick pay except for those who hold executive positions.

Benefits may also include, when affordable, group insurance (life, accident, health), a retirement plan, profit sharing, bonuses, stock ownership, employee discount of ten to fifteen percent on merchandise purchased from the store.

For stores that are open seven days every week, you may choose to give everyone a day off each week, or you may choose to give a weekend off periodically. Of course the number of working hours and remuneration for overtime must meet government regulations.

Payroll taxes

Withholding tax is withheld by the employer from wages due as indicated on a chart provided by the IRS. The employer pays FICA (Federal Insurance Contributions Act), which is social security tax, matching the amount the employee pays and for which the employer deducts from the employee's wages. The total amount of FICA—that paid by the employee and employer—and the withheld withholding tax are sent to the government, usually via a local bank, accompanied by the proper forms and according to federal instructions.

An employer's identification number is required on all employment tax returns. It is obtainable from your regional IRS by filing Form SS-4. Federal withholding and social security taxes are reported on Form 941. The return for each calendar year is due on the last day of the following months: April, July, October, January. Remittance of taxes may be required before the due date of the return. Deposits are accompanied by Form 501, "Tax Deposits Withheld Income and FICA Taxes," and made at a bank authorized to accept them. The smaller the amount of tax liability, the less frequently you must make deposits. If all deposits were made on time, you may file Form 940 on or before February 10 following the close of the year.

Workers' compensation and federal and state unemployment taxes are paid annually, accompanied by the proper forms. You must pay unemployment taxes if you paid wages of $1,500 or more in a calendar quarter or had one or more employees on at least some portion of one day in each of twenty or more calendar weeks, either consecutive or nonconsecutive. If taxes exceed $100 for any calendar quarter and any preceding calendar quarter, you must deposit tax with an authorized bank within one month following close of the quarter, along with

Form 508, Federal Unemployment Tax Deposit Form. An annual return is filed on Form 940 on or before January 31 following the close of the calendar year for which the tax is due. You file on the calendar year even if you operate on a fiscal year.

You should have a record sheet for each employee stating name, address, telephone number, social security number, rate of pay and for what period, overtime pay, number of tax exemption claimed, amount of deductions for FICA, withholding taxes, insurance, pension and savings plans. This information is used for quarterly and annual reports to the IRS. At the end of the year, the employer forwards a W2 form to the IRS and to each employee, which states how much was withheld from the gross wage.

The employee must sign an IRS W4 form authorizing withholding tax from his wages. When there is more than one employee, payroll checks should be written in the payroll check register, and it is practical to use a check of a color different from those written for other store expenditures. Business form companies have checks with stubs especially for recording important information for payroll records. The one-write system of such checkbooks saves time and mistakes. At the end of each month, all payroll figures are totaled and recorded in the general ledger. See employee payroll sheet in Fig. 6-4.

Name of employee

Address

Telephone number

Date of birth

Social Security Number

Pay rate and for what period

Overtime rate

Withholding taxes

Number of tax exemptions claimed

FICA contributions

Other deductions

    Insurance

    Pension

    Savings plan

Weekly or monthly payroll sheet summary

Date	Employee	Gross salary	FICA	Federal withholding	Other withholding	Total net

Fig. 6-4. Employee Payroll Sheet.

Firing

Before firing an employee, refer to that person's job specifications, and then look at the application that he had filled out when you hired him. How well do they match? Did he exaggerate, or lie—stretch or even bend the truth?

Despite this analysis, you may decide that he was not right for the job. Firing is in order: An unhappy assignment, but the buck stops at the door of your office; you must do it yourself. Save face for him. Don't embarrass him. Have him sit down in your office and discuss with him why you no longer require his services. Then let him talk and tell his side of the story. Listen carefully. There may be a lesson in what he tells you.

Tell him the reason for your action, unless it was because of dishonesty or other gross behavior, in which case you open yourself to possible court action.

As an employer I found it preferable to end employment immediately, even if it necessitated payment of salary in lieu of notice. When an employee gave notice himself—quit the job—I usually used the same procedure if it seemed bad for employee morale to have the person continue in the job.

If it's a matter of a satisfactory employee being "laid off" because of internal reasons, slow business, change in need of an employee for a particular job, a written reference describing his commendable qualities will help that person find employment elsewhere. The sooner he gets another job, the less unemployment compensation you will be responsible for.

Make an immediate record of the employee's work for you and why you ended employment, and of the statements made by each of you during the final session. Such record may become useful if unemployment compensation comes into question, or if another employer calls you for references.

If possible have the employee leave this session with a feeling of good will toward the store and the boss.

Ways to prevent theft

"Pilferage" is petty theft of supplies and merchandise by an employee. "Embezzlement" is taking funds.

You have reason to suspect internal theft if there is a marked decrease in cash sales, an increase in cash returns, or an inventory shrinkage.

To avoid back-door thefts, flatten all discarded containers, and never allow employees to park their cars near the back door or leave the store from an unattended back door.

The owner of the store should audit all bank deposit slips, handle all mail, and supervise all merchandise returns. Sales slips should be checked to verify chronological order of their numbers. Take a periodic physical inventory of merchandise and office supplies yourself; be cautious about overtime work by employees who are in the store alone after closing hours; keep reserve office supplies locked up.

Care must be taken in giving out store keys. Have all keys stamped "DO NOT DUPLICATE." Have a separate key for the office. There may be an occasion when an employee leaves your employ without returning the store key, or loses a key; in such instances you may consider it wise to change all store locks.

It's permissible to add the estimated value of pilferage as an operating expense in the cost of doing business.

If there's a robbery

Caution your staff that should there be a robbery, they are not to fight with or chase the robber; they are to stay in the store, and when he leaves they are to call the police and write out a description of the robber.

To protect the staff from robbery outside the store, make bank deposits by having different people go to the bank at different times of the day and in different cars.

7

Setting customer policy

GENERAL POLICIES ARE PART OF YOUR BUSINESS PLAN. THEY ARE YOUR GUIDES in all matters of management procedures and practice. Policies express the image of the store, the goals you strive to reach, your merchandise and its price range, the ads you write for the newspaper. It is therefore logical that the owner is the policymaker and makes decisions expressed in all policies, written or unwritten.

They may be general policies such as store hours affecting the whole business. Or, they may be specific policies affecting portions of the operation such as rules related to merchandise returns. Specific policies reflect general store policies. In this example, the general policy of the store might be "No Sale is Final." The special policy is that all merchandise is returnable, whether or not accompanied by proof-of-purchase sales tickets.

The specific policies enable the entrepreneur to make prompt decisions in the light of already established general policies. They are blueprints for behavior that govern your decisions and hold you to the line when faced with specific problems. A certain latitude for judgment in individual cases may be permitted, but you are cautioned to restrict the range of allowable deviations from the rules.

Policies must be definite and consistent. They lose their reason for being if they are flexible. Instead of breaking a rule, change the policy. Be confident that you and every staff member will interpret policies as established. Don't you be the soft guy. They have been made on the basis of careful consideration of all factors and must be understood and enacted by every staff member, without supervision of the owner. You made the rules, so there is no question they meet with your approval. Thus armed, employees can act with confidence when faced with decision-making. Emphasizing a particular policy gives superiority over competition. For example:

"The Customer is Always Right"—his complaints are always treated as valid.

"There Never Are Interest Charges on Your Monthly Statement"—we don't charge interest on charge purchases.

A retail store at its outset, before the door is open to customers, should formulate not only its general policy, its goals, but specific policies, particularly those relating to customers and personnel.

Know your customers

The success of your store depends on your developing a loyal following—customers who look to you first when they are in the market for something in your category of merchandise. You may have buyers but not regular customers. You should know why they shop with you in the first place—for mark down prices, excellent service, instructions and lessons in using your product, or your money-back policy.

A small store does not need a computer to identify its customers. The alert manager is on the sales floor constantly; she knows what is going on. She should know when customers are pleased or displeased.

Make shopping in your store a pleasurable experience. In years past, Marshall Field and Company in its Chicago loop store served coffee in the outer lobby to early bird shoppers who arrived before the store opened.

Ways to handle complaints

Give customers what they want and what they expect to find in a store like yours, regarding both merchandise and service. Be alert to customer complaints rather than being on the defensive. Listen to dissatisfied customers rather than regarding them as cranks or nuisances.

Be quick to own up to your own errors; don't argue or alibi, and thank the customer for bringing the matter to your attention. Should the complaint come over the telephone, promise to call back when you get all of the facts, and then do call back with a complete explanation. You, the boss, must be on the side of the customer—his ally.

Seemingly minor events can create unpleasant shopping experiences—for example, the salesperson who gives priority to the customer at the other end of the telephone rather than the one standing on the other side of the counter.

Should a clerk be the buffer who receives all complaints, make very sure he is doing it your way, and with courtesy and efficiency. The good reputation of your business is in his hands.

One of my most prized customers evolved because of the way my store handled a rainy day complaint. A bright blue store shopping bag had faded onto her raincoat. The coat was sent to the cleaners by the store and returned to the customer with a complete refund of the price of the coat, which was several years old.

Deciding on affordable services and prices

Being honest with a customer gives him good value in exchange for his money and the service he has a right to expect, plus a little bit more than that. But you must be able to afford all such extras. Service does not always mean money outlay. It could mean clean and inviting lounge rooms, wash rooms, and dressing rooms; clean sidewalks and show windows; comfortable places to sit, uncluttered aisles, and good lighting.

You might give better guarantees than your competitors because your sales are final only when your customers are satisfied. Trinkets for the children, candy or cookies at the checkout counter, large packages delivered to a loading ramp— there are many little ways that you say "welcome" and "thank you" to your customers.

Establish a definite discount and mark down policy; for example, a yarn shop gives a ten percent discount based on past purchases of a certain amount; a hosiery store gives a pair of hosiery free for every twelve purchases; a grocery store issues rain checks to disappointed customers when the store runs out of advertised sale items.

Price is based on your store image and overhead expenses. Some of the free services you provide may require study of what you can afford. The fewer customer services you provide, the lower your affordable sale price can be.

Retail business does not allow for much variance in price, particularly of nationally advertised brand merchandise. Cutting your prices to meet competitors' lower prices may be hazardous. You must make your fair profit. Instead, give your customer reasons for buying these items from you and not from merchants who cut prices—for example, carry a wider assortment from which the customer can choose, provide gift wrapping, or offer free out-of-town as well as local delivery. A list of customer services appears in Fig. 7-1.

In other words, if you have a reputation for being expensive, counterbalance it with emphasis on the added value you provide. It may be that the item sold involves additional labor costs—for example, in a fabric shop, yard goods need measuring and cutting, and the help of an experienced salesperson; on sale days you require extra trained personnel. Cutting your prices in order to be competitive could result in an unprofitable margin. When considering cutting prices to match competitors' prices, bear in mind that they may be using them as leaders, marking up other items to absorb the loss.

Pricing is a complex subject and is more fully covered in Chapter 10.

Setting a merchandise return policy

Have a definite policy for customers wishing to return merchandise, taking into consideration what your store can afford and your competitor's policies. It's a service that you give to customers, and you may set your own rules. Type of merchandise—furniture and heavy appliances, perishables—governs your policy in this regard.

Gift certificates

Gift wrapping, mail wrapping

Merchandise returns

Merchandise delivery

Rest rooms, ladies lounge, drinking fountain

Shopping carts, baskets, tote bags

Charge accounts, deferred payments, no interest charges on charge account purchases

Personal checks, credit cards of other businesses accepted

Bulletin board for local notices

Notices in show windows

Layaway plan

Guaranties and warranties in addition to those of manufacturers

Evening and Sunday shopping hours

Free coffee, snack bar, beverage vending machines

Alterations

Installations

Instructions and lessons

Parking, valet service, taxicab telephone

Automatic teller machine

Playroom and playground with attendants

Wrap- and parcel-checking service

Fig. 7-1. Some Customer Services.

You can expect customers to read a sign posted by the cash register stating the rules. In some instances, such as the sale of mark down merchandise, you might write on the sales slip, "Not returnable or exchangeable." Rules might be:

1. returnable under all circumstances—no questions asked
2. returnable when accompanied by the sales slip
3. returnable within a specified number of days
4. exchange only
5. credit on another purchase
6. neither cash nor charge credit—all sales are final unless the merchandise is faulty

Setting an open account credit policy

Open account credit means that the customer may make charges whenever making purchases. Should you use open charge accounts, you must set up a policy: to whom, for how much, and on what terms. Accounts are usually due for payment within thirty days of purchase. There are no carrying, service, or interest charges for accounts that are paid when due. In setting interest charges for delinquent or unpaid accounts, you must observe state regulations. The way to avoid bad (uncollectible) accounts is by choosing the right customers in the first place, and establishing their amount of credit.

For opening a charge account, application blanks usually request such information as place of employment, amount of income, credit references. Credit records of applicants are available to members of local credit bureaus.

If your collection losses are less than two percent, you can be rather lenient with good customers who are late payers; but if losses are over five percent you have been too lenient. Close follow up on accounts that become past due is necessary. If an account is delinquent, you or your bookkeeper must make sure that no more credit is given to that customer. The longer delinquent accounts are carried on your books, the greater likelihood they will not be paid in full.

Advantages and disadvantages of charge accounts

There are both advantages and disadvantages to a policy of charge accounts.
Advantages:

1. You have faith that the buyer will pay bills when they come due.
2. You might not make sales to this customer otherwise.
3. It is psychologically easier for a customer to say "charge it" than to count out cash.
4. You acquire a monthly mailing list, and without extra cost, you can keep your regular customers informed of sales and new merchandise.
5. Even though it requires time-consuming paperwork and collection problems, it encourages regular customers.

Disadvantages:

1. Accounts receivable tie up business funds.
2. You will need working capital of about 1.5 to 2 times the credit sales.
3. Added expenses and costs include interest on working capital invested, collection costs for delinquent accounts, debts that are never paid, costs of bookkeeping, postage, and stationery.

Charge account recordkeeping

Keep accurate files of items purchased, amount, date, and payments. Have sales slips for charge accounts (and lay away purchases) in triplicate, and keep the "triplicate" copy in your own files. When a check is given to pay an account, write that fact on the face of the check, to differentiate it from checks written at the time of purchase.

Other credit media

You may give customers credit without the burden of collections by honoring credit cards issued by major banks: Visa, MasterCharge, American Express, and others. Your profit is reduced by the amount you pay for this service; it may be around five percent. You lose some identity with customers because you don't have them on your mailing list when you send out store news, but you avoid the ill will of customers to whom you would not give credit. Credit cards are particularly useful if you have tourist trade.

You can also give credit without having to handle collecting by selling your accounts to a factoring agency. Using this method gives you less than 100 percent of the value of the sale, but it gives you your money at once and with certainty. Should you use this method of collection, inform your customers of the source of billing.

For high-priced merchandise such as furniture, cars, and appliances, conditional sales contracts may be written. The purchased item serves as collateral; title to the item is passed to the buyer when payments are completed.

Setting a collection policy

Mail monthly bills promptly, preferably a day or two before the end of the month. Have a plan for collecting overdue bills—a handwritten note on the late bill as a reminder, then a friendly telephone call, and that followed by a letter. If these do not bring results, send a certified letter as legal notice of your intent to sue. Your final recourse is court action; you can use small claims court, where you do not need an attorney.

Collection agencies are ordinarily of minimal value; they are expensive and create ill will.

Be tenacious but cautious in dunning delinquent payers. Do not threaten. Consult your lawyer as to what you may and may not do. Remember, a creditor may not close an account because the customer refuses to pay an account which he or she has indicated to be in error.

Dealing with customer checks

You do not have to take a check, even if the customer has what he may consider proper identification. However, when refusing to take a check, do not use a statement that may be considered discriminatory, such as, "We do not accept checks written by college students" or "We accept checks only from people living in the neighborhood." You may say, "We do not accept checks written on out-of-town banks" or "We accept credit cards but not personal checks."

A check should have written on the face whether it was for merchandise, lay away payment, or charge account payment. All checks should be for the exact amount of the transaction.

What to do about shoplifting

"Shoplifting" is thievery on the part of "customers." It accounts for considerable merchandise shrinkage. To keep it under control, constant vigilance by the store staff is important—train employees in this regard. Stores may use such devices as surveillance mirrors, electronic noise activators attached to merchandise, television cameras, and security guards. Eliminate aisles with high barriers such as shelving and tall hangracks. Bookstores should avoid the use of the library type of "stacks", tall shelving arranged on narrow aisles. If at all possible, the entire store interior should be in view from every location in the store.

Neither customers nor staff should be permitted to leave the premises from an unsupervised rear door; this may create somewhat of a problem for stores with parking lots at the rear.

Be aware of common tactics used by shoplifters—putting on garments and walking out of the store; coming in as a team of two, one to distract and one to steal; switching price tags; using such hideaways as handbags, baby carriages, and umbrellas.

Watch out for loiterers. Count items taken into dressing rooms. Keep small valuable items, such as cameras, expensive billfolds, and jewelry behind counters or in locked cases.

To apprehend a shoplifter you must see him take the item, be able to identify it as your merchandise, and be able to prove it was not paid for. False arrest does not necessarily mean arrest by a policeman, but may mean preventing the person from pursuing his normal activity as a customer. If you chase him, be sure that he had not abandoned the item; otherwise, you may be in great trouble.

Building bridges to your customers

The monthly mailer is an excellent medium of communication, keeping customers posted about your store's happenings and plans. Communicate with your customers in a variety of other ways—via newspaper, radio, television, personal telephone calls of congratulations as well as with information about new merchandise, and thanks for visiting the store whether they bought anything or not.

8

Interior layout and design

SHOPPING IN YOUR STORE SHOULD BE A PLEASURABLE EXPERIENCE, SO KEEP your customers in mind in creating a pleasant atmosphere. The advice of an expert in designing retail store layout will save you time and money, but such professional advice is useful only when it meets your own requirements and goals: to maximize sales, be convenient for your customers, save the time and energy of the work force (including you, the owner-manager), and discourage theft.

From the outside looking in

The impression you make on your customers starts with the store exterior—the sign on the front and the awning over the front to shade the show windows from sun damage. Show windows, important for displaying your merchandise, can also express the image you wish to create.

Consider the nature of your business as you visualize its exterior. The store front should identify it as representative of its type of business. The luxurious exterior of an exclusive shop would turn away someone looking for a variety store or an antique store, and vice versa.

A building in a prime location on Main Street remained empty for a long time because of its facade as a bank building with cement pillars on either side of its entry door.

Entry steps are a psychological barrier in addition to making the store inaccessible to the physically handicapped. Entrances should facilitate quick flow of traffic—self-opening doors or two swinging doors, one for inbound and the other for outbound customers.

The outside sign, carrying the name and perhaps the street number, should be bright, conspicuous, and eye-catching, garish only if your merchandise is garish. Its purpose is to attract attention and alert those who pass by, either on foot or by car, that you are here. The show window's purpose is to arouse interest in the store and encourage passersby to enter. The attractive display lets customers know what you carry.

Not all retail stores have show windows. Those in shopping malls frequently have none; the space on either side of the entry door is used for displays similar to those in show windows.

Window displays can hold a little of everything—a few specially selected items, or a combination of the featured display and a taste of the rest of the store's items. When you display merchandise of current interest plus merchandise of continuing appeal, you are telling the whole story of what is for sale in your shop.

Men's stores often carry a little of everything. If their appeal is to the "carriage trade" they display a little of everything more subtly—a mannequin wearing a suit, tie, shirt, handkerchief in the jacket pocket, shoes, socks, and sometimes even a hat. Variety stores and stationery stores display a sample of almost everything they sell. Women's fashion stores usually display a few specially selected items.

Change the displays to keep them interesting to pedestrians and to clean the windows, the need for which will be determined by the area. Jacobsons had as its neighbors two cement plants and a railroad station; they were good for business with their continuing payrolls, but destructive to clean air, so the windows were washed daily and cleaned weekly.

Jewelry stores are best served with traditional small show windows at eye level. Their displays usually are removed at the end of each business day for safety's sake.

You will be asked by customers for permission to put signs in your window. Establish a policy in that regard. You probably will give negative response to political signs.

Ceilings should be light in color in order to give proper light reflections. Low ceilings, especially in small areas, may give customers the feeling of being closed in. High ceilings create a more roomy atmosphere. Use soundproofing when acoustically necessary.

Use color in walls, floors, and fixtures to create desired effects. Lighter colors are more pleasing and have light-reflecting ability as well. Warm colors are red and yellow. Apparent size can be increased by the use of receding colors, such as blue or white, or decreased by the use of advancing colors in deeper shades.

Get expert advice about lighting from local public utilities. Basically, there are two types of lighting; fluorescent and incandescent, each with advantages and disadvantages. Fluorescent lighting has a high level of light intensity and is relatively inexpensive in consumption of electricity, but color is not always true, an important matter to consider when planning a men's store or fabric shop. Incandescent bulbs are the kind you use in your home; they give warm, lifelike tones to merchandise and are good to use where you want to highlight an item.

Use lighting that is both functional and decorative in the quality that fits your business. Subdued lighting in a boutique may be pleasing but is not functional—colors are difficult to judge, and too many shadows are created. Some lights are better to work under; the staff's comfort adds to its efficiency. But comfortable lighting does not necessarily enhance merchandise and compliment customers' complexions.

The walls may be painted, paneled, tiled, wallpapered, or mirrored. Choose a covering that is durable and attractive and also meets your decorating budget. Consider the initial cost and upkeep. You could provide a bulletin board as a service to customers who make requests for window space.

Via window displays, you personally might promote the state fair, community events such as the high school homecoming parade, your own special sales, promotions, anniversaries, and national holidays.

Sidewalks must be clean and free from ice and snow. A small carpet just inside the door during inclement weather is appreciated by customers. In Japan, I recall seeing holders for customers' wet umbrellas at the entrance; should you wish to adopt this custom, you might want an attendant to ensure that umbrellas are returned to their own owners.

Inside the store

Once inside, the customer should have a clear view of what the store has to offer. And in planning your interior, don't go second class because yours is a small store. Make it as pleasant and attractive as you can.

The floors should be safe for walking, and should look safe. They can be of wood, cement, tile, linoleum, or carpeting. The choice depends upon suitability to your customers. But avoid slippery floors that are highly polished or look as if they are slippery.

Jacobsons had two kinds of customers—women who were fashion conscious and men, some of whom might have come straight from their farms or jobs in a nearby cement plant. The women's department was carpeted, and the floors were easy to walk on in all kinds of weather; the men's department had cement floors, so that customers never needed to be self-conscious about grimy work boots.

Keep the interior design as flexible as possible with racks and even walls that can be moved from place to place, and shelves that can be moved up and down. Well-designed fixtures, considered as an investment, should be selected with an eye to growth of the business. However, for a new store, the price of such fixtures is of prime consideration; they may be rented, bought secondhand, or improvised by using gas pipes for hangracks and folding tables as display counters. Even large companies have put themselves out of business by their initial over-expenditure on eye-appealing offices and stores to impress the public.

The business determines the interior decor. In a men's store, a club atmosphere is achieved with wood paneling and display fixtures. In a bakery, gleaming white walls look spotless and sanitary.

Making the most of the space

Draw up a floor plan, the object of which is to put floor space to its best use—merchandise in the right place at the right time. Good layout encourages multiple purchases, impulse buying, and economy of salespeople's time and energy. Analyze the store activities involved—the customers, salespeople, office staff, and stockroom personnel—and then determine location. The objective is proper display of merchandise for maximum sales, customer comfort, convenience, and service. Planning with the staff in mind calls for an arrangement that provides efficiency of operation.

Trade associations have designed model layouts best suited to the needs of particular businesses, such as variety stores, stationery shops, and bookstores.

The plan is based on customer traffic flow. The degree of priority of placement of the merchandise follows a definite pattern: first, right front; second, center front and right middle; third, left front and center middle; fourth, left middle; fifth, back.

In a store with more than one floor, the higher the floor, the lower the selling value.

Customers usually turn to the right when they enter a store; attract them to the left as well, and to the rear. "Destination shoppers," who go directly to what they want, expect quick service when making their purchases. Arranging staples and convenience items to the left and toward the back requires that they pass other merchandise—tempting displays of impulse items. The drugstore places over-the-counter medicines, toothpaste, and the pharmacy counter in the rear of the salesfloor. In shoe stores, the "staple" styles are in back of high fashion styles.

People usually leave by the left, a good place for the checkout counter.

Businesses used to have shelves behind counters, with merchandise out of customers' sight and reach. When I was in high school, I worked one summer in a department store at the handkerchief counter. Expensive handkerchiefs were kept tucked away in a drawer.

Businesses now are following the lead of self-help stores by using their type of layout. However, if yours is not a self-help store, your staff should be expected to be salespeople and not just package wrappers; they are there to serve the customers.

Put merchandise in easy reach. In luxury stores, displays are kept low; in discount stores, for safety's sake, many items are placed above eye level. Expensive items should be highly visible but physically inaccessible.

Merchandise may be arranged by size, by line (manufacturer's labeled items), by price. Men's suits usually are hung by price; however, a mixture of price lines trades up the purchases. A large stock of one style on one rack cheapens the item, and is inappropriate for high-fashion apparel stores.

All sizes in one style is practical for displays of shoes, electrical appliances, and home furnishings. In a shoe store, stocking by sizes saves salesmen's time, but increases the amount of time it takes to do inventory to find what to order for fill-ins. Jacobsons kept men's shoes by style number, and count was taken every Thursday night so that orders could be sent to the supplier on Friday.

Draw up a plan within each department, putting the best sellers at the front, the slow movers at the back. See Fig. 8-1 for suggestions on how to move slow-selling items. Have a fixed location for regular selling departments, and also have a place for temporary display of mark down items. Putting a few impulse items near the checkout counter reminds customers of their needs—batteries, pens, films, and candy bars.

Housekeeping

Good housekeeping is a must—aisles clear of boxes, sidewalks and windows clean, glass counters free of fingerprints, boxes on shelves lined up, dresses and coats brushed and buttoned. Your maintenance person is an important member of your staff who does the floors and windows, but whose work does not include attention to the merchandise. The first duty of the sales crew each morning is to dust counters and arrange merchandise and displays.

Don't permit trash to accumulate; empty cartons are a fire hazard and an incentive for pilfering. Set the custodian's work hours either before the store's opening hours or at closing time, depending upon your own choice.

Discouraging theft

"Robbery" is stealing by force. Avoid robbery by having well-lit parking lots and an illuminated store interior during closing hours. Leave no cash in the store after hours, and keep cash register drawers open. Keep no valuables in show windows overnight—there may not be insurance for such displays as jewelry and furs. Have an alarm system at doors and windows. Join with other merchants in the area to hire a merchant policeman for weekends and nights.

If you plan to do your own housekeeping and stockwork at first, the work space should be where customers can see you and where you can see the salesfloor, the entrance to dressing rooms, and the entire store.

Displays that are traffic obstacles

Colored lights

Displays next to best sellers

Signs saying "special of the day"

Special-colored price tags

Special discounts for quantity purchases

A 1¢ sale—first one regular price, second one 1¢

A one-day-only 50 percent discount

Fig. 8-1. Suggestions for Moving Slow-Selling Items.

9

Marketing strategies

MAYBE PEOPLE WANTING BETTER MOUSETRAPS WILL BEAT YOUR DOOR DOWN NO matter where you are to buy your mousetraps, but not to buy anything else. No matter how kind you are to your employees, how cooperative you are with your Main Street colleagues, how excellent your merchandise—unless you get customers into your store to buy your wares, you won't remain in business very long. You must convince people it is to their advantage to be your customers. And after that you had better deliver what you promised, or they won't be back.

Advertising is promotion—sales strategy. Its goal is to let people know you are in business, where you are, what you sell, and benefits of buying from you—to get them into your store the first time and to keep them coming. Advertising for your regular customers is the newsletter that keeps them informed of your new merchandise. It also reaches out to potential customers; it whets their appetite for owning products they did not know they needed or wanted. And it attracts them to what promises to be a pleasurable experience. Used correctly, advertising is your most important part of salesmanship. It can be the potent growth factor of your operation. It is mass selling as the prelude to individual selling. Exclusivity of merchandise is somewhat of a fallacy. More than likely your merchandise can be bought elsewhere, even in your own neighborhood. Advertising is to create the desire to use *you* as the purchasing resource. If competitors in your area carry your same brands, it's up to you to differentiate your offering in some way—price, services, credit terms, delivery, or variety of selection.

Advertising is the adjunct to the eye-to-eye relationship between you and the customer when, in response to your ad, he comes to your store, looks at the product, and listens to you explain its good features.

For hints on how to plan and budget advertising, see Figs. 9-1 through 9-4.

1. Have an advertising plan.

2. Have an advertising budget.

3. Focus on your own target market.

4. Stay within your budget.

5. Advertise only money makers.

6. Use advertising allowances by vendors.

7. Use free advertising.

8. Have a sustained program.

9. Coordinate all advertising with your buying schedules, store displays, informed sales personnel.

10. Avoid general copy that helps competitors sell the same items.

11. Analyze periodically records of ads, dates, cost, weather, sales results.

Fig. 9-1. Economy Measures That Make Advertising Affordable.

There are many ways to advertise

Advertising takes a variety of forms. Some may be too expensive for you to consider; some are cost-affordable, some are free. Advertising is the printed promotional material that appears in daily newspapers, weekly shoppers, monthly magazines, quarterly mailing pieces. It is the billboard and bus-stop bench. It is plastered on the outside of the bus. It is the eye communication of television and the ear communication of radio. It is the show window display and the in-store mannequin on which a tag displays the outfit's price.

In Jacobsons we used many small signs which my husband called "talking signs" that pointed out the features of the item to which they were attached. These signs were professionally hand printed. Sloppy signs tear down the store's image.

Budget

Selected media for advertising

Monthly advertising schedule

Promotions and specific plans for them

Periodic review of all advertising to determine (a) strengths and (b) weaknesses

Window display program

Interior display program

Public relations program

Training the staff

Fig. 9-2. The Advertising Plan Includes.

Month	Last year's budget*		This year's budget	
	Gross sales	Advertising expenses	Gross sales	Advertising expenses
January	_____	_____	_____	_____
February	_____	_____	_____	_____
March	_____	_____	_____	_____
April	_____	_____	_____	_____
May	_____	_____	_____	_____
June	_____	_____	_____	_____
July	_____	_____	_____	_____
August	_____	_____	_____	_____
September	_____	_____	_____	_____
October	_____	_____	_____	_____
November	_____	_____	_____	_____
December	_____	_____	_____	_____

*For a new business, use trade statistics or an estimate.

Fig. 9-3. Annual Advertising Budget.

Type	January Budget Actual	Year to date Budget Actual
Media		
newspaper		
shopper		
radio		
television		
others		
Promotions		
displays		
contests		
fashion shows		
mailers		
others		
Advertising expenses		
salaries		
supplies		
postage		
stationery		
others		
Total		

Fig. 9-4. Media Advertising Budget.

Advertising is the Fourth of July parade and other community activities in which you participate and the word-of-mouth enthusiasm of satisfied customers. It's the yellow pages of the telephone directory, the shopping bags and boxes with your name imprinted that serve as "sandwich man" advertising as shoppers walk through the streets carrying their purchases.

During the Christmas season, a Des Moines, Iowa, department store gave their shoppers large, attractive paper tote bags in which to carry purchases. Bags carried in the mall proclaimed purchases made in that particular store—expensive bags but inexpensive advertising.

You must decide what media are best for you: what merchandise is best advertised on television with its potential for demonstration; what's best in the yellow pages where people look for specific information; what's best in the newspaper with its daily, timely circulation. A door-to-door circular would hardly be suitable for announcing the arrival of a new jewelry store on Main Street, but it would be productive in announcing the opening of a new bakery. Your objective is to find the most effective media to present a distinct image of your store, differentiating it from the competition and convincing the public of its superiority.

Matching the media to the customers

Targeting the market is the prelude to all of your advertising plans—matching the media to the customer. This is your number one advertising economy measure. Advertising is expensive: to pay its way it must bring results. Know your customers, actual and potential; and study various media to determine those that will be most efficient in reaching them.

You cannot afford not to advertise. Adapt the old saying, "You have to spend money to make money" to, "You have to spend money correctly to make money." And don't spend all of your money in one place because only one medium will not do the job. Answer these questions before choosing the media that are right for you:

What is the maximum audience for the least cost? Does it reach my kind of customers? Is it exciting?

Is it affordable?

Does it have frequency and flexibility?

Is my best bet long copy, such as in a newsletter, or short copy, as on a billboard?

Most small retailers find their best advertising media are handbills, newspapers, weekly shoppers, radio, and direct mail. Those with wider markets use magazines, television, and billboards.

Use handbills

Small stores often find handbills effective. They are easy to prepare. For a modest cost and in small quantities you can prepare your own copy, illustrating it with paste-ups. Sometimes, distribution might be a problem. Handbills are wasteful when they are not read and could become litter. Local ordinances may interfere with this kind of distribution. However, hand-distributed circulars can explain a lot about your store and merchandise to neighborhood residents.

Use direct mail

Mailing pieces are available from vendors, or you can work with professionals to design your own. They are excellent as a means of keeping customers informed of timely items and store events. You need accurate and up-to-date mailing lists, which you can formulate from your own customer lists, rosters of local organizations, and newspaper public announcements such as marriage licenses and building permits; or you can buy them from advertising agencies, which will also prepare mailers and send them out for you. Postal cards can reach periodically a select group of customers, keeping them informed of special store events.

Jacobsons had a specially designed postal card. It often was sent out in comparatively small quantities to notify pinpointed customers of particular new items. The salespeople used them to reach their own customers, and we found them more effective than using the telephone for such purposes.

The cost of mailers includes the insert, mailing paraphernalia, and postage. To save on mailing costs stay within the weight limit of a letter. Get a permit to use bulk mail. Use lightweight envelopes that can be opened without breaking a seal for postal inspection.

The value of direct mail is that it goes directly to potential customers and to "occupant" in selected areas. When inserted in monthly statements to customers, there is no additional postage expense as long as the weight is not increased into another price category. (Statements must be mailed first class, not at bulk rate, and therefore are not subject to postal inspection.) Its weakness is that mailing is costly when used for a large market, wasteful when not done creatively. Mail has become an overused medium. It is saturated with advertising pieces, not only from stores such as yours, but even from purveyors of such products as gasoline and credit cards.

Use billboards

Billboards and marquees can direct traffic to your door, and messages can be changed periodically. But their messages are perishable, and maintenance can be difficult.

Use the yellow pages

The yellow pages have wide advertising use because everyone has a telephone book. People are ready to buy when they look through the pages for specific product resources. This advertising medium is particularly productive for specialty businesses such as those selling children's apparel, shoes, radios, and televisions, and shops that sell services as well as items. Their weakness is that ads are costly, and you may feel compelled to match competitors' big ads.

Use classified ads

If you have a store in a small town close to a metropolitan area with a large circulation newspaper, classified advertising is an inexpensive way of widening your trade area. People read the classified ads when looking for particular items. An economical way of keeping your name before the public is to use a good eye-catching lead phrase in a classified ad that uses as few words as possible but with enough information to transmit your message. Classified ads are priced by the line.

A small furniture store was able to compete with the cut-price full-page ads of a large furniture store by running a number of little ads, featuring specific items and prices in the classified section of every local Sunday newspaper.

Use radio and television

The weakness of radio and television is that the message perishes instantly, in contrast to printed advertising. An advantage is that a friendly and persuasive voice establishes rapport, and a broadcast presented in a conversational manner conveys sincerity and urgency.

Radio advertising is fairly inexpensive. Messages are prepared easily and there need not be any production costs. The message is immediate and flexible—it can be changed quickly. There can be interesting sound effects. The ad can be repeated several times during the day at minimal cost. Radio stations usually have a special packet of spots, for example, fifty spots over five days for a set rate. A station's programs determine its audience, a matter for consideration when choosing where to advertise.

In your station selection, you probably will find that smaller stations have lower advertising costs, and they may be more inclined to give more personal service. When placing an order for a radio commercial you must be sure to specify whether you want AM or FM if the station you select has both. In spot announcements, feature something special, and be sure to include your address and telephone number. Keep the copy short, interesting, and to the point. Use action words and those that create images.

Television is the Cadillac of advertising. It comes the closest of all media to personal selling. It combines sight and color with motion and sound. The product or service can be demonstrated in a realistic setting. However, you are pitting your advertising talents against those of national advertisers with huge budgets and advertising staffs. Furthermore, you may be paying for more coverage than your business warrants.

I took great pride in my weekly fashion shows on television until I realized they may have been entertaining, but they were not bringing customers to the store. I switched to fundraising fashion shows for churches and local charitable organizations, a contribution to the community which proved to be lucrative as well for Jacobsons.

Except for the wide difference in cost, TV and radio advertising are similar. Rates depend upon the number of commercials you contract to buy and the times at which your advertising will be aired. You are buying time instead of space, as when you advertise in a newspaper. Along with fees paid to broadcasting stations, there are preparation costs. You can choose to write your own radio copy, but you will need professional help to prepare television ads, the success of which depends on visuals. For either broadcast medium, take advantage of the help available from station staffs.

Local cable television is gaining in popularity as an advertising medium. Its merit to a small store is that you can target your audience through a specific cable channel in the geographic area of your choice. The price is much less than that of regular television, and you pay for advertising only in the area that reaches your potential customers. The disadvantage is that it can deliver only in a metropolitan area.

Use the weekly shopper

If customers live within a radius of about five miles of the store, advertising in the weekly shopper may be more effective than in the daily newspaper, and certainly less expensive. As its name indicates, people review ads in the shopper to get shopping information.

Jacobsons found the weekly shopper one of its most effective advertising media. It reached both pedestrian and vehicular traffic. Our voice in placement of the ad was respected by the shopper manager, who also helped write and illustrate the ad.

Use the daily newspaper

For a business whose market is nationwide, television and periodicals may be logical advertising choices. For a business whose potential market is encompassed in a single state, a newspaper with statewide circulation might be the choice.

The strength of newspaper ads is their coverage because almost everyone reads the newspaper. People respond quickly to newspaper advertising, and the message is considered good for about a week. Their timeliness makes newspapers valuable for special promotions. Their weakness for the small business is that they may cover a wider area than is profitable for the store. And since rates are related to circulation, they are expensive. If you have a choice of newspapers, compare the cost per reader. A vendor's cooperative advertising service often helps pay for the ad, and also provides the copy and the pictures.

Writing effective newspaper ads

The purpose of an ad is to sell a product, so it must attract customers by developing their interest, convincing them, and getting them into the store to buy the item.

To write copy, you must have confidence in your own operation and merchandise. Know why they are superior. Know their strong features and describe them in your advertising. Your unique qualities differentiate you from your competitors, which is why your regular customers stay with you; for example, your hardware store might open at 7 A.M.; or you not only own the drugstore, you are the pharmacist. Maintain a consistent personality, and above all, express everything in good taste.

An ad must attract attention. The headline especially must be eye-catching, and express a single major idea. And a well-written ad motivates the reader to look beyond the headline.

The ad should be easy to read and understand. Write the way you talk. Emphasize the positive. Be brief. Use short sentences, action verbs, and exciting adjectives. Be specific. Stress benefits for the customer such as value and price, and emphasize the importance of buying now. Use enticing words such as "free," "special offer," "homeowners," "career women"; instead of "reduced prices," use "$100, now $39.95"; rather than "best service," feature "two-hour service."

Exaggerations arouse suspicion, as do misleading statements. There are truth-in-advertising requirements that define what you can and cannot do. Be careful to conform to state and federal regulations.

A cut-price store advertised certain popular items at greatly reduced prices. When customers went to buy them, they were told they were sold out, but that the store did have similar items of a superior quality, which were at a higher price. The cut-price store had the rug pulled out from under the feet of this unethical practice. A competing store, my client, publicized this procedure in time to avoid being hurt in its Christmas selling season. The newspaper that had run the ads was a cooperating force.

Use a simple layout, with pictures emphasizing the dominant product and expressing the idea in the headline. Do not use pictures that reproduce poorly—a line drawing may be better than photographs.

A newspaper sales representative will usually help you set up ad copy, placement, and size. Timing is important, and the representative may suggest the most effective advertising days for your kind of business. In some areas it's preferable to run the ad just before payday of the area's large industry.

Regarding ad size, space should be large enough so that it's not overcrowded, and there's an allowance for white areas. A small ad can get lost unless properly placed. Some merchants prefer to use four ads, a quarter of a page each, rather than one full-page ad; others choose large ads to make an impact on the reading public. Some run several ads in daily succession, then skip a period.

Placement of the ad on the newspaper page is rarely the prerogative of the advertiser, and there may be premium rates for particular positions. Choose the best sections: news, household, and fashions. Aim, if you can, for upper location. The third page is considered to be choice by some advertisers.

Try direct promotions

Promotions put spice in the store calendar. They may relate to specific events such as an anniversary, a holiday, remodeling, or a special sale. You may use enticements such as coupons, prizes, giveaways, refreshments, discounts, window displays, and balloons. Colorful signs and banners highlight the event and attract public attention. Some sales promotion incentive ideas are listed in Fig. 9-5.

Contests

Premium offers

Discounts

Free trial offers

Sample sizes

Coupons

Games with prizes

Two-for-one offer

Family rates

Senior citizen rates

Student coupons

Credit points to students based on their grades

Fashion shows

Trade-in old for new

Open house for Christmas

Open house for store opening

Open house promotions
management and staff greet customers

Trunk showings

Package wrappings with store name and logo imprinted

Store services
layaways, gift wrapping, evening and Sunday hours, refunds

Telephone
sales force tells customers of new items

Unique gift wrapping

Customer register
useful for mailing list

Selective mailing list

Thank you letters to customers

Post card mailings to customers

Fig. 9-5. Sales Promotion Incentives.

The grand opening of your store is an important time for a promotion. Tell your vendors, and they may contribute display pieces and giveaways. Invite local florists to participate. Send invitations to other merchants, the chamber of commerce, service clubs, city officials, newspapers, radio and television stations.

Join with other merchants in the area—for example, if a sidewalk sale is an annual event, put it in your plans.

Promotions must be preceded by careful planning, making sure that you'll have the advertised merchandise shipped to you in time and in sufficient quantity. Send special notices to your regular customers. If you plan to have extra staff, make sure it is properly trained.

You may find it worthwhile to use an advertising agency for a particular promotion. It is an expensive luxury but may be an excellent investment. Ask for an estimate; it may be less costly than you think. Be prepared to pay for the artwork and copywriting as well as for the service.

Set up a way to measure the success of the promotion. Keep a record of the advertising program and cost, number of coupons redeemed, other expenses, which items sold best, gross sales, and anything such as weather that might have influenced traffic. Also keep a record of the days the promotion was held because some days of the week might be found to be better than others.

Cash in on cost-free advertising

News releases are the way to get free advertising in the newspaper—difficult in large cities but easier in small cities. The "Home" section of the Sunday newspaper even in a large city may run a story about a new product you are carrying, or about the opening of your new store. You might call on the news editor of your local paper and ask him what stories he would consider newsworthy, and whether he would accept a 4 x 5 photograph with the story. Contact him when you add a new person to your staff, or when you schedule a fashion show for a local benefit.

Local radio and television broadcasting stations carry hometown news. You may use institutional ads that promote the local high school's sport events or the Boy Scout troop's paper sale.

Extra customer services such as free parking, gift wrapping, baby sitting, and evening shopping hours are worth advertising. Publicize them and remind your customers of them frequently.

Participate in indirect promotions

Participation in community projects is indirect advertising. The results are hard to measure, but they are as important as product advertising. The average store loses about twenty-five percent of its customers annually. For the store to survive, these customers must be brought back or replaced. Indirect advertising has as its objective replacing customers who have left, enticing new customers, and retaining present ones. It keeps the public aware of your store and its merits. Favorable public relations are established when a business participates in events that promote its business area, for example, charity benefits and community improvement projects. Acting as a sponsor of the Memorial Day parade, contributing shirts for the softball league, inserting in your regular newspaper ad a small "boxed" announcement of local high school happenings—these are some of the ways a business expresses concern for the neighborhood.

The store's location determines the focus of its public relations policy. On Main Street of a small city it is the entire life of the city; in a shopping mall, cooperative efforts with the other merchants; in a shopping strip, the people in the neighborhood.

Such public service is the way a merchant might thank the community for support. The community owes you nothing, but you have a responsibility to it. Participation in local events is not an act of charity; it carries its own rewards, including your recognition as an esteemed member of the community.

Set a store policy concerning contributions

It is true that merchants are harder hit than almost any other business or profession by solicitors for nonprofit organizations. You are approached frequently by good customers who are difficult to turn down. Advertising in every high school annual in your county can kill your advertising budget. Don't say "no"; just pick out a small space so that you can say "yes." And charge it to publicity or contributions, where it belongs. It is not advertising; nor is an institutional ad actually advertising. Advertising should get specific response: people coming to your store to buy.

Set the amount you can afford in your annual budget, and get a receipt for all contributions. When contributions are made in the form of merchandise, keep a record of the dollar value since they're usually tax deductible.

Good will and advertising

Advertising is nonpersonal persuasion—printed words and pictures, voices on the radio or television. Word-of-mouth is your very best and least expensive advertising. Satisfied customers promote repeat business. Conversely, disgruntled customers spread a reputation that could be costly. You and everyone else on your salesforce who answers your telephone are very much a part of your sales strategy. Special attention to your method of handling complaints is warranted given the cost of avoidable unpleasant situations. Impress this upon your staff. Daily customer relations that are friendly and confidence-inspiring, courteous telephone manners—all of this should be emphasized in frequent staff meetings. "The customer is always right" might be antediluvian in the big stores, where clerks are package wrappers and the big boss is secluded in an office on the tenth floor, but it's the prized motto of the little store. You, the owner, are always there to set everything right. Good will is the reputation a store earns by how customers are treated, management's attitude, and merchandise quality and reliability. Integrity is your prized ingredient.

The motto of the great nineteenth-century John Wanamaker was, "What we advertise, we must do." It holds good today. Basic to your advertising messages is the image of your store as a business with quality products, efficient service, guaranteed satisfaction, fair prices, and salespeople who are friendly, pleasant, and self-assured because they know the merchandise.

Constructing an advertising budget

The advertising budget starts with the advertising plan. Advertising has been described as a business investment. Certainly it is a sales-building investment. You waste money by advertising too heavily, but halfhearted effort is worthless.

Look first to anticipated sales volume to determine what percentage of that amount you can afford to spend on advertising expenses, including supplies, stationery, and postage. If you have purchased an established business, last year's records will indicate what you can anticipate for the coming year's sales. As a newcomer in the field, go to the statistics of trade organizations to find average sales in your kind of business and what percentage of sales was spent on advertising. The average figure for retail stores is three percent and perhaps twice that amount for opening a new store. Some businesses use a fixed-dollar basis, figuring how much of income from each unit goes to advertising.

As a guide, look to what others do, but your own circumstances must govern. For example, more advertising is used by stores that emphasize price, have less favorable locations, or are expanding or facing strong competition. A percent of sales may not always be the prudent method. When business has fallen off, cutting advertising to conform to reduced sales income might be an error.

To get your monthly budget, multiply your total anticipated annual sales by the advertising percentage you have decided on, and divide this by twelve. Then adjust this figure to your own business. For example, if April contributes eight percent of the year's sales, plan to spend eight percent of the advertising budget in April. An exception is the Christmas season, which contributes as much as twenty-five percent of your sales; plan to spend Christmas advertising money in October, November, and December.

10

The ABC's of buying, maintaining, and managing inventory

WHAT IS INVENTORY? FOR THE RETAILER, IT IS THE MERCHANDISE HE HAS FOR sale. For the manufacturer, it's the materials used in the manufacturing process and the completed product. Some retail businesses such as bakeries both manufacture and sell their products. For all merchants, inventory is a crucial factor in operation of their stores.

Inventory is money. It's money in the form of merchandise that will be converted into dollars when sold. Inventory turnover is the number of times a year the money from the sale of inventory is used to replenish the sold inventory. At the end of the fiscal year, the inventory on hand is part of the business assets.

It is also money in the form of merchandise sitting idle on shelves or in the warehouse. Unsold merchandise may be a drain on cash flow because of the expense of storage and maintenance, investment which has not brought in a profit return. It's the interest on money that was used to buy slow-moving items, and the storage expense for obsolete, nonsalable items. And there is also the profit that could have been made if the money had been invested otherwise. It has been determined that inventory sitting around idle costs twenty to twenty-five percent above its original cost.

Careful inventory control increases sales for profit by minimizing slow items that eventually are sold at a mark down or scrapped because of obsolescence. The longer that inventory takes to flow through the business, the longer that money is tied up and unavailable for other purposes.

Poor management of inventory results in business losses. Too little inventory means loss of sales. Overbuying is equally disastrous—too much inventory or unprofitable inventory that ties up capital. This could lead to excessive borrowing entailing interest expense. Conversely, efficient management of inventory increases working capital without the need to borrow money. The market value of inventory in many businesses is short. It is measured in days for the produce in food markets. It is measured in weeks or a single season in fashion shops. Paying bills depends upon conversion of inventory into dollars.

Buying for your market

The buyer must concentrate on the most consumer-desired types of merchandise and patterns of purchase in his own neighborhood. In some areas people are taller or shorter than average, and this changes the usual buying formula of purchasing heavier in the middle sizes and lighter at each end of the size scale. Color preferences are also regional. I found that adult customers in my apparel store avoided orange because it was the color of high school football uniforms and jackets.

Fashion influences fabrics. It influences not only skirt and trouser lengths, but also tie and lapel widths. Fashion influences outerwear as well as lingerie, foundation garments, and sleepwear. It determines the style of scarves, handbags, jewelry, and gloves. Fashion governs furniture, floor coverings, table linens, automobiles, bicycles. The selling life of merchandise for the most part is limited. Cameras, television sets, typewriters, and computers become out-of-date when new models hit the market.

The fashion buyer, no matter the price category, must know market trends and be alert to fashion changes. In my shoe department, tiny children dictated what brand of shoes they would allow the salesmen to put on their feet, reflecting the power of television advertising.

The store's buyer should be a people-watcher. Good viewing arenas are the television and movie screen. She should know consumer preferences—what they're looking for when they come into your store.

Good sources of fashion information are the New York markets, trade publications such as *Women's Wear Daily*, newspapers, and advertising in fashion magazines. Every business area has trade journals and other publications which keep buyers informed. An astute buyer visits other stores—call it snooping, if you will—and examines the displays. He asks the sales representatives who call on him what other stores are buying.

Going to market

Buying takes two forms: merchandise replacement and beginning-of-season needs, which may also include replacement of staple items. Your major buying is in this latter category and sets the pattern for later replacements.

Beginning-of-the-season buying quantities depend upon anticipated sales for the next three to six months. In an established business the buyer looks to last year's figures; in a new business the buyer couples the statistics of like businesses with his own good judgment, and with caution.

Quantity depends entirely on inventory records of an established business; carefully-kept records tell you what to buy, from whom, and in what size, color, and quantity. Even new stores should be aware of seasonal variations and buy accordingly, and they should take a positive view of inevitable slack seasons. Inventory policy is reflected in slack months by reducing inventory accordingly. When significant variations are apparent, the storekeeper should attempt to adjust not only the buying but also the operating expenses. For example, use part-time employees only during the busy months—November, December; Have all employees take their vacations in July and August if they are the slack months. And feature special sales and promotions to increase sales in slow months.

Fashion business requires careful planning of buying because of seasonal fashion changes. Fashion has a short season, but buying should be modified by the fact that an assortment of merchandise for selection by the customer is important.

The selling pattern of your own store determines what items are profitable— six percent of your inventory may produce twenty percent of your sales. The fastest-selling items may produce the highest percentage of sales but not necessarily the highest percentage of profit. Constant analysis of your records determines what is selling the fastest and what is most profitable.

Avoid factory close-out, job-lot, and promotional buying unless your store is set up for that kind of business. If someone overstocked or miscalculated in manufacturing those items, don't you miscalculate by getting the supplier off the hook. Don't over-order just to get quantity discounts. Such buying will get you in trouble unless you are in the market for quantity stock. Be wary of salesmen's samples; they usually are all of one size—a small size; and if the merchandise is defective or shopworn, or the packaging is shabby, which is often the case, it's not returnable to the factory or may not carry a warranty.

I was once assigned by SCORE to counsel the owner of a new men's sportswear shop. As I entered the shop I was struck by a display in its most prominent location of lightweight, shortsleeved sweatshirts. This was in November—a very cold November. The owner told me he had bought them at a greatly reduced price and could not understand why they were not selling at such a bargain price. Much of his inventory budget had gone into this purchase, leaving very little money for investing in Christmas gift salables.

It's imperative to have stock at the right time and in the right quantity. Capital may be limited; therefore, inventory levels must be in proportion to capital available to pay for it, while providing sufficient merchandise to meet the market's demands. Reorders are governed by the promptness of suppliers to ship, keeping in mind that adequate supply and assortment are necessary to maintain inventory levels that will produce the necessary cash flow. Reorders by mail or by telephone, verified by mail, are methods for reordering between markets and visits of factory representatives.

Low inventories result in loss of cash flow because of lack of sales. Beware of overstocking on slow items; neither must you understock on fast-moving items. Inadequate inventory and stockouts are as harmful as overstocks.

Many of these admonitions as to what to buy, how much to buy, and where to buy relate to a business already in operation; but the wise new entrepreneur sets up buying plans aware of possible merchandising pitfalls. A false start can tie up capital at the very outset.

Selecting your suppliers

Who will provide you with the merchandise for stocking your store? You may look to the manufacturer or to a merchant wholesaler who buys items from the manufacturer for resale to the retailer. Jobbers sell the merchandise of a variety of manufacturers, and often specialize in odd-lot sales. They are good resources for small stores, such as children's, gift, variety, and hardware stores, since they make available small quantities of a variety of brands. They are accustomed to working with small stores and value them as customers.

Resident buyers are middlemen, agents of wholesalers, and are in business for themselves. Their customers are, for the most part, small stores that rely on professional resident buyers to do some of their buying for them. Resident buyers have buying power; they can order large quantities at a reduced price and distribute their stock among small-quantity buyers.

In selecting your suppliers, study their merchandise carefully according to its profitability and its suitability to your store. If your store image is that of prestige merchandise and high fashion, look for fashion leadership in your supplier. If your image emphasizes quality classic merchandise, look for that resource. Ask yourself whether brand names are actually important to your customers: are they even aware of brand names? Is it efficient to buy from suppliers who sell to your competitors? Remember, however, the benefit of advertising by "The Big Store" when it carries the brands you carry; the prestige of carrying those brands will rub off on you.

You can learn about suppliers by studying trade journals and advertisements displayed in them, and by studying the merchandise in competing stores. In large cities, you'll find brands listed in the yellow pages. And you may go to the trade shows, the markets where wholesalers come together in one area or center several times a year to do business with retailers.

Look for suppliers who provide dependable service and who appreciate the smaller stores' business. Know their distribution policy and their quantity-of-purchase requirements, credit terms, and shipment methods.

For those from whom you decide to buy, keep an evaluation system—prices, discounts, shipping records, interest charges, policy for return of damaged or unsatisfactory merchandise, completeness of shipments, and adherence to specified shipping dates. Where the selling season is short—for example, for Christmas toys—shipments past the stipulated date jeopardize sales. The supplier may be inclined to provide large stores in your area with off-price merchandise at the height of the selling season, or honor their orders ahead of yours.

Will the supplier pay part of your advertising costs, do national advertising, or be available for cooperative advertising? Will he provide you with mailing pieces, display signs, display racks?

Although manufacturers' recommended prices generally are honored by retailers, an astute retailer may sometimes get price advantage by having the privilege of returning unsold items—actually a form of consignment buying.

Making the buying decisions

Before going to market, make a chart of what to look for and a system for considering new items and new suppliers. For staple merchandise buying, have a chart with you indicating where you are open to buy, the number of units and amount of money to invest in each category; subdivide each classification as to its particular requirements. A good overall policy is to establish a price range and a budgetary allowance for each category of merchandise. Establish a percentage of your buying money to purchase what you know will sell, what you think will sell, what you hope will sell. And then stick to the percentages.

Have some idea of where to buy, how much to buy, minimum quantities required by suppliers, and how to place the order. Don't use too many suppliers. You need their cooperation and their confidence in you as their customer in your city. When you visit the booth of the supplier you've selected, write a sample order, then shop around and review the order before making the final commitment to buy. Check competitive prices and delivery dates of competing suppliers.

Some businesses may choose to go directly to the manufacturer and do their buying in the factory showroom. It's sometimes easier to get advantageous prices that way.

Come armed with figures

Your pre-buying homework, wherever you buy, is to establish a budget for the season—a basic stock list, which you have compiled by using a unit control system, leaving enough money to buy during the season. Caution is your own responsibility in judging quantities. "Let the buyer beware."

Your own salesperson is invaluable, once you have decided on your supplier. He knows what is selling in your area, and he will advise you of fast-selling items. A good salesman is "on your side." He knows his success depends upon your success; he will guide your buying and be less likely to oversell.

In writing the order, state the date of the order, the store name and address, terms (discounts), completion date for accepting shipment, color, size, quantity, price, total cost of purchases, insurance, shipper, and any special arrangements. The price usually is not negotiable. However, you may be able to make special arrangements for quantity buying, closeouts, dating, interest rates on deferred payment dates, and advertising expense.

A word about the larger world

Going to market is to attend trade shows where many manufacturers and wholesalers display their wares. You may be able to do much of your buying in your own store when salesmen call on you. However, markets offer the opportunity to view many suppliers' wares and keep you informed of new items and buying trends. There are regional markets and also big markets in New York and other big cities. It's educational to attend the big markets occasionally. You probably will find it best to use your regional market for your main buying. A great advantage is that your own salesperson will be there, and he knows your store; the merchandise he shows you will be pinpointed saleswise to your particular section of the country.

The disadvantage of buying only in regional markets is the danger of look-alike merchandise because in targeting the market in the particular area of the country, the supplier representative may have narrowed the selection to appeal to your competitors. Also, it's more likely that the salesperson will overload the buyer at the trade show than when he works in the buyer's own store and analyzes store potential.

You may feel intimidated by the salesperson at first. You may feel the rush of having so much to do in so little time, with other buyers crowding in. But you will be spending your own money. The welfare of your store is in your own hands, and never so crucially as when you are spending so much money on next season's merchandise. Work with the supplier for the benefit of your store.

Pricing policy

In retail stores, profit figures are based on retail price. "Gross profit" is the difference between your cost and the selling price, which is known as "mark up." "Profit percentages" are determined by profit divided by the retail price. You buy a lamp for $20, sell it for $40—your gross profit is $20; divide that by your selling price of $40 and you get the markup or profit percentage of fifty percent. The total cost of your merchandise for the year is $60,000; you sold it for $100,000; your gross profit is $40,000, your gross profit percentage is $40,000 divided by 100,000, which equals forty percent.

If you are planning to sell $100,000 of merchandise a year and your normal turnover is 3.2 times, you'll need from $28,000 to $30,000 of retail sales to make this volume of sales; you have made a net profit of about 3.7 percent.

For brand name merchandise, stores usually accept the manufacturer's price suggestions. In fact, the manufacturer expects it. For other merchandise, set a policy to govern the percentage of mark up. Keep in mind that the cost of inventory is the money paid to suppliers, plus the money paid for its delivery to your store, the interest on the inventory investment, depreciation, obsolescence should it not sell, pilferage, internal handling costs, storage, insurance, and taxes. Inventory carrying cost is actually ten to twenty-five percent above the price you paid for it to the supplier.

Decide whether your price will be above or below market price, but set it to cover the cost of doing business, or average that amount when you price some items as leaders; add the profit percentage you expect. Reorders may be more expensive than the original order price, and yet you may feel obligated to refrain from increasing the price. Grocers are prone to raise the price on items already on their shelves when the wholesale price increases; the same is true of hardware, automobile parts, and office supply stores as well as other businesses governed by supplier catalog prices.

Fashion shops and highly serviced stores may require a larger mark up in order to balance the large mark down before the season ends and while the remaining items are still salable—or to pay for services overhead. For that reason, many such stores avoid popular brands because competition prevents marking above suggested factory prices; stores get around this situation by having their own labels on merchandise rather than factory labels. See Fig. 10-1 on pricing merchandise.

Establish a mark down policy. For example, your first mark down on dresses may be twenty-five percent of the retail price, then 33¹/₃ percent of the original price, then fifty percent. Determine what products draw crowds when placed on sale. Is there a specific time when competitors have sales and when customers expect sales, for example, Columbus Day and the day after Thanksgiving? Is it better to have one clearance sale when you make drastic price reductions? Are you affected by competitor's mark downs?

The ideal is to sell inventory so fast that you collect from your customers before you have to pay suppliers, but few storekeepers experience that. Fashion establishments usually have to pay for Christmas merchandise in September or October. Charge customers may not pay for Christmas purchases that they made in October or November until January, February, or later; the time lapse between when your bill is due to the supplier and when your customers make their payments may be six or seven months.

Inventory management

It is necessary to maintain inventory levels consistent with requirements of the business—to have just enough stock to meet customers' requests. Merchandise was bought to be converted into cash from sales. This is what is meant by inventory control.

Inventory turnover records tell you whether or not the business is prospering. The higher the turnover rate, the more sales you are producing from a given investment. For example, a turnover of four times a year indicates twice as many sales from the same inventory as a turnover rate of two.

A new store bases its figures on the experience of similar stores in estimating rate of sales and inventory level, and to determine whether the rate of sales will be a satisfactory return on investment. It acquires these figures from government reports and such statistical sources as Robert Morris Associates' Statement Studies.

Mark up as percentage of selling price	Mark up as percentage of cost
50%	100%
40%	66.67%
30%	42.86%

Fig. 10-1. Pricing Merchandise.

A new store should have an opening inventory about ten percent above the normal stock level. After the first year in the life of the business, as a buying guide the estimated inventory for the year is achieved by using this formula:

1. opening inventory for the previous year,
2. plus additions to the inventory during the year,
3. less deductions.

The additions include purchases from suppliers and returns by customers. The deductions are the merchandise sold, pilfered, returned to suppliers, and scrapped as nonsalable.

Many items require a basic stock—a safety stock—an amount sufficient to accommodate regular sales with a reasonable assortment. This means maintaining a monthly planned inventory level. The estimated annual inventory divided by twelve tells the store buyer the average monthly supply that's needed. Such figures are tempered by seasonal sales. For items sold year-round, it's necessary to base purchases upon average monthly sales, allowing for year-to-year growth. The entrepreneur keeps account of unfulfilled customer requests. Perhaps he ran out of the item last year or there were unforeseen shipping delays. "Open to buy" figures are adjusted to a forecast of increased sales, a conservative percent of increase commensurate with the percent of sales increase.

If the store policy or budgetary requirements are to maintain a five-week supply of staple merchandise and the actual inventory shows you have an eight-week supply, you must reduce inventory or slow up on your orders. If inventory is a four-week supply, more should be ordered to avoid loss of sales. The object is to keep inventory as low as possible and turn it into cash as rapidly as possible.

Inventory control depends on recordkeeping—a record of the business stock and the history of its inflow and outflow. Maintain accurate, up-to-date records in order to prevent shortages. Records are a database for decision-making regarding buying. Good business means maintaining inventory levels sufficient to meet requirements, replenishing in anticipation of demand, not waiting until you are out of salable items and thus losing sales, and reordering best sellers. A certain amount of gamble is involved, but gamble tempered by entrepreneur's good judgment—based not on a casual memory of past experience but on actual facts as recorded in the inventory story. Stock records tell you what you have; sales records tell you what you need. However, the entrepreneur must take time to study these figures prior to any buying and must bring the information to market.

By constant study of investment-control data, control is accomplished by prompt correction of imbalance—prompt elimination of overstocked items through markdowns, sales throughout the department, merchandise donations to charity taken as tax deductions, sales to outlet stores, sidewalk sales, and scrapping—in other words, clearing shelves of obsolete merchandise.

The sales record plus the stock record are tools of efficient inventory management. Together they comprise the statistics that help you make sensible buying decisions. They also point out past mistakes or miscalculations because they show the stock that did not sell. Insufficient sales of items on hand might suggest the need for store promotions, changing displays more frequently, moving the item to another spot in the store. Notations on sales records will tell you why certain items did not sell—boots did not sell because the winter was mild and dry, or raincoats and umbrellas sold very well because of an unusually rainy spring.

If stock is excessive when demand declines, it has to be cleared, even at sharply reduced prices. Styles change, products become outdated and lose their sales appeal. Slow-moving inventory ties up capital. It's equivalent to taking the same amount of cash out of your bank account and placing it on a shelf where it will gather not interest, but dust. Not only is that amount of working capital frozen, the stock occupies valuable space which would be better utilized for fast-moving items. The longer one delays in disposing of obsolete inventory, the more rapid is its decline in value. Eventually it becomes worthless. Styles are unpredictable, and they change; sometimes they never get off the ground. Be prepared to take mark downs. Defective merchandise, and (when possible) discontinued styles should be returned promptly to the supplier.

Inventory control systems

Inventory control is an established system that provides a means for constantly reviewing what is on hand, what is on order, and what needs to be ordered. It provides a periodic physical count. It may be a dollar-control system as in a meat market or a unit-control system in a men's store.

The inventory control system must be concise. It should take a minimum of the owner's time to keep it current and accurate. Office supply forms usually require adjustment to particular business needs. Plan to design your own forms to set up a management tool for your own merchandise assortment—an efficient, practical system of recording and reporting quantities in specific categories.

Some items might require no formal records. A visual method, done weekly, is a quick method you might use for very fast-moving items; you see what is left on the shelf. A very small business may find it practical to judge inventory needs merely visually. An example of this would be a meat market with a quick turnover of merchandise; in such a business, which makes almost daily purchases, dollar-control is adequate. On the other hand, a bakery is also a manufacturing business, and a unit-control system is required to anticipate its needs for flour, sugar, and packing boxes. Perhaps in your business, the bin system would be most practical—in which a running count is kept and attached to each container, and a refill order is written when the supply is down to a certain amount. This might be best for certain items carried by a hardware store.

Each store must establish its own basic program for each category or staple. In Jacobsons' men's shoe department we took a count every Friday of fast-moving styles and telephoned our refill order every Monday morning. For unit-control of fast-moving style items, such as slacks and jackets, we wrote mail orders stating style number, color, and size because we did not want vendor substitutions.

Some stores streamline their merchandise control by using what is described as A B C control.

A items are expensive, high-fashion merchandise which is stocked in minimum quantities and reordered frequently, or as the need arises. Stocktaking is frequent, usually weekly, and reorder weekly. The wholesaler serves as the retailer's warehouse.

B items are controlled routinely. The maximum stock is determined and the quantity reordered periodically based on past sales. A salesperson is assigned to biweekly stocktaking.

C items include not only sales merchandise but also office and wrapping supplies, items used in manufacturing or repairs. Bins or shelves stock the items, and one in each category is marked "last container" to indicate when it's time to place a reorder, always taking into account shipment time.

A small store may find it practical and accurate to use a physical-count inventory system combined with a perpetual inventory system. The most accurate record is the perpetual inventory system, in which every item of merchandise is tagged with a two-part sales stub indicating the manufacturer's code, date of receipt in store, and price code. In the file is a card or record for each item, on which is listed the manufacturer and his item style number, color, size, and price. The quantity and date of receipt are recorded. As merchandise is sold, information is taken from the sales stub, or from the sales slip that has a record of the necessary information. The card shows the movement of the item—sales, returns by customers or to the manufacturer.

Color coding is sometimes useful—colored tags or colored ink on white tags—to indicate the season purchased; for example, red for winter, green for spring, yellow for summer, orange for fall, blue for carryovers from last year.

For bookstores, a card file is practical, using cards of different colors for paperbacks, clothbound, best sellers, and staples. Each card lists title, author, publisher, price, quantity ordered, date of order, and sales. Bookstores having the option of returning unsold books may use a little, unobtrusive color dot on the back of the volume to indicate when it's returnable to the vendor.

Whatever the system, the purpose is to know what is on hand, what is on order and not yet received, and what needs to be ordered—in other words, to pinpoint open-to-buy quantities based on the store's own experience, as recorded on its fact sheets. Successful inventory management requires timely, accurate information for decision-making purposes. It is more than an inventory; it is the system set up for control of merchandise flow. It is a stock record and also a sales record. It calculates where you are open-to-buy, at what time, and in what quantity. It points out items that sell fast, slow, or slower. It prevents overstocking of slow-moving items. It dictates turnover but only at a profit. The result is a good assortment of merchandise in controlled quantity.

You are prepared when you go to market, and you are prepared when a factory representative shows up in your store without an appointment and expects to write an order.

How to take inventory

Merchandise inventory is the record of stock on hand. It is actually a record of goods which have not sold, but which must be kept on hand in proper quantity for the purpose of being sold. The periodic book inventory is arrived at from dollar figures: beginning stock, deductions due to sales, returns to vendor, pilferage and nonsalability, and the final on-hand figures. But for actual buying information this record is inadequate. The record must be item-by-item in appropriate classifications—price, color, model, and vendor. This requires a record form custom-designed for the specific business.

Records are made when items are received. At that time, buyers' orders and shippers' packing slips are checked with the merchandise, which is examined and, if defective, put aside to be returned to the vendor; and this information is recorded. Sales of merchandise and returns by customers are recorded from sales slips or price-tag stubs, as described.

In addition to paper records of inventory, a physical inventory should be taken periodically to be sure quantities on hand equal those shown on inventory records. Paper records are then adjusted to reflect any differences that show up in the physical count. Unless you know exactly what you have, you are not prepared to fill in the gaps caused by pilferage, faulty receiving procedures and records, customer returns, and unsalable items not returned to vendors for credit.

Only through such periodic physical count can there be a true picture: What is actually salable, what is damaged or obsolete, and what is missing. Only when the manager participates in the process of handling, counting, and recording can she determine where corrective measures should be used to control overstocks, pilferage, merchandise damaged by careless handling, failure to return defective merchandise to the factory; to follow up on returned merchandise to suppliers to assure credit; or to judge suppliers themselves. By handling the merchandise herself, the manager can discover that fast-moving items are in too-short supply.

Figures 10-2 and 10-3 describe a unit control and perpetual inventory systems, respectively.

Stockroom procedure

Merchandise as it arrives in the store should be unpacked promptly and checked with its enclosed packing slip. The record of its receipt is also indicated by circling on the buyer's order form:

6   #1834 toasters
12   #8386 blenders

The merchandise should be examined carefully. Defective items, to be returnable, usually require the vendor's permission. The response to your letter of request is usually a sticker to be placed on the return package.

Notations relating to merchandise returns are made in a stockroom record book and checked periodically to make sure that credit is received for such returns. Periodic review of order forms should also be made; merchandise that has not been received by the due date may be cancelled at the buyer's discretion.

Stockroom supplies include price tags and tickets, packaging materials for mailing purposes, return forms in duplicate for enclosing with items sent back to vendors, and return address stickers. For pricing merchandise, a marking machine or a rubber stamp is imperative; never use a pen or pencil.

Each price ticket and tag should tell, in addition to the price, the wholesale cost, date of receipt, and vendor. The number code for the price might be:

A D O G I S T R U E
1 2 3 4 5 6 7 8 9 0

The code for $12.98 is ADUR; for $4.75, is GTI.

Instead of writing January 2, 1989, add 2 to each number - 243101.

You might also use a code letter for the vendor - A for Hay Bolton Company, B for Smith and Sons, C for Dodge, Inc.

New merchandise is now ready to be stored carefully until its transfer to the selling area.

Date _____
Men's long-sleeved shirts
$12.98 to $14.98

White

vendor	basic	on hand	on order	open to buy
Babcock	____	____	____	____
Contemporary	____	____	____	____
Donnelley	____	____	____	____

estimated sales for three months ____

estimated needs for three months ____

on hand ____

open to buy ____

blue

vendor	basic	on hand	on order	open to buy
Babcock	____	____	____	____
Contemporary	____	____	____	____
Donnelley	____	____	____	____

estimated sales for three months ____

estimated needs for three months ____

on hand ____

open to buy ____

Fig. 10-2. Unit Control System.

Item _____

Cost per unit $ _____   Selling price per unit $ _____

Date	On hand during month	Received	Total	Sold during month	Returns*	Balance	Inventory count
Jan	——	——	——	——	——	——	——
Feb	——	——	——	——	——	——	——
Mar	——	——	——	——	——	——	——
Apr	——	——	——	——	——	——	——
May	——	——	——	——	——	——	——
June	——	——	——	——	——	——	——
July	——	——	——	——	——	——	——
Aug	——	——	——	——	——	——	——
Sept	——	——	——	——	——	——	——
Oct	——	——	——	——	——	——	——
Nov	——	——	——	——	——	——	——
Dec	——	——	——	——	——	——	——

*returns by customers or to vendors
 a card or page for each item or category, detailed as to size, color, etc.

Fig. 10-3. Perpetual Inventory System.

Part III

Financial recordkeeping and analysis

Part III

Financial recordkeeping and analysis

The art of bookkeeping

RECORDKEEPING IS VITAL TO BUSINESS SUCCESS. SOME RECORDS ARE NON-financial, relating to activities of the business and its management style—inventory, insurance, payroll, and depreciation. The heart of the business is its financial record, the accounting system. That is the barometer of the health of the operation. As the decision-maker of your business, you must refer to financial records as your working tools. They are critical when preparing tax returns or applying to the bank for a loan. To be trustworthy, they must be accurate and up-to-date. Not only must you be accurate in compiling these figures, you must be equally diligent in using them. They should help you in conducting your business and also in planning the future. They must be easy to understand and simple to maintain.

This chapter is about bookkeeping, the process of writing down all business transactions in an orderly fashion. Accounting, the science of interpreting the bookkeeping records into a form that will give the financial status of the business, will be discussed in the following chapter.

Bookkeeping is a formula for keeping score of business finances. It is accepted universally as a system for recording income and expenditures. You are expected to follow it with blind trust, not questioning its theory, just following the pattern.

The bookkeeping system for you

The best bookkeeping system for you depends upon the size of your business. At the outset you may choose to be your own bookkeeper—the least expensive method of recordkeeping—and to use an accountant to set up your books. You can in turn teach an employee how to post business records. Your system should be simple enough for you or your employee to keep up-to-date on a daily basis, with the accountant to make tax returns, monthly, quarterly, and annual statements. The plus of keeping your own books, receiving periodic analysis from a professional source, is that you're continually alert to the status of your business.

There are various packaged bookkeeping systems available in office supply stores. Among them are forms in which each transaction is recorded with only one entry, which includes writing the check or making the bank deposit. You may choose to use a computer agency's services as well as an accountant on a periodic basis. You may wish to design your own system. Whatever your decision, care must be taken to avoid oversimplification of entries. There should be a record of daily sales transactions—income and expenditures—and a summary. Information must be quickly and easily accessible, and usable for taxation, insurance, and intelligent business operation.

Single entry and double entry explained

There are two types of bookkeeping methods: single entry and double entry. In the single entry system, a daily recording, diary style, is made of income and expense items, and a monthly summary is prepared of receipts (income) and disbursements (expenses).

In double entry bookkeeping, the pages of the entry book—the ledger—have two sides for each account. The left side of the page is the debit side, and the right side of the page is the credit side. Debit is left; credit is right. Don't look for a meaning in their names. You could call them Jack and Jill, or Humpty and Dumpty. Debit does not mean increase or decrease; it could mean either, depending upon whether it is a debit in assets or a debit in liabilities or capital. When debit is used in assets, it is to increase assets—the left side. When debit is used for liabilities or capital, it is to decrease liabilities or capital.

Every debit must be balanced by a credit, and vice versa. Each entry on one side must be balanced by a corresponding entry on the other side. The total of the debit posting should equal the total of the credits.

In double entry bookkeeping this is how accounts are increased or decreased:

type of account	if transaction increases account	if transaction decreases account
assets	debits	credits
liabilities	credits	debits
net worth (capital)	credits	debits
income	credits	debits
expenses	debits	credits

Equity accounts (capital) have the opposite characteristics of asset accounts. They are increased by credits and decreased by debits. Liabilities, a form of ownership of your business by those to whom you owe money, as well as owner's equity, increase on the right side. Revenues (profit) increase ownership equity, so they show increase in the right side entry.

Don't be discouraged or dismayed by this confusing dissertation. The system can be established by an accountant and can be followed routinely by you, thus giving your accountant the information he or she needs, in the language accountants understand.

The cash recapitulation sheet

The simplest bookkeeping method is to use the cash recapitulation sheet as the daily record. It's also helpful when clearing cash drawers daily. The total of these daily figures are recorded on its sheet for the month. The totals for each month are recorded on the monthly summary sheet.

For this type of recordkeeping, every check that is written has recorded on its stub or face the type of transaction, for example, advertising, salary, rent; this expedites its entry in the proper column of the monthly summary sheet. The monthly totals provide the figures for you and your accountant to strike a balance periodically.

See Figs. 11-1 and 11-2 for daily and monthly cash recapitulation data. Figure 11-3 provides guidelines to summarize all daily records.

Keeping the records straight

Record books—journals and ledgers—are used to enter transactions. There may be one ledger and a number of journals.

The journal is the first accounting record of business transactions; all of the necessary information about all transactions is recorded in chronological order, day by day. There are a number of different types of journals; the one commonly used is the general journal.

The ledger is the second record of transactions; it gets its recording information from the journal, grouping and summarizing the transactions, for example, rent, wages, and accounts payable. The transferring of data from journal to ledger is called "posting" and usually is done monthly.

The journal and ledger pages are different: the journal has space for a description of the transaction, usually titled "description"; the ledger summarizes and totals. Monthly journal totals are posted to appropriate accounts in the ledger, entering also the ledger number with every journal entry. There may be the following journals, as necessary:

Sales
Purchase
Cash disbursements
Cash receipts
Notes receivable and payable
General journal to record all items not otherwise recorded in specific journals

Date

(front)

Cash drawer

Daily cash report

1¢

1. Cash on hand end of day

5¢

2. Cash on hand beginning of day

10¢

3. Net cash increase

25¢

4. Paid out

50¢

5. Total cash accounted for

Coins total

6. Received on account (subtract)

Currency

7. Cash sales (gross)

Checks

Register reading

Total for deposit

Cash sales

Total retained in register

Received on account

Total cash at end of day

8. Total cash rung up

9. Shortage (line 8 less 5)

10. Overage (line 5 less 8)

Total cash paid out

(back)

Merchandise purchases

Purchases _____

_____

Wages _____

_____

Supplies _____

_____

Maintenance _____

_____

Advertising _____

_____

Rent _____

_____

Utilities _____

Refunds _____

Others _____

Fig. 11-1. Cash Recapitulation Sheet.

Date	Cash sales	Disburse-ments	Purchases	Wages	Supplies	Mainte-nance	Adver-tising	Etc.	Total
1									
2									
3									
4									
5									
6									
7									
8									
9									
10									
11									
12									
13									
14									
15									
16									
17									
18									
19									
20									
21									
22									
23									
24									
25									
26									
27									
28									
29									
30									
31									
Total	___	_____	_____	____	_____	_____	____	__	

January

Fig. 11-2. Monthly Annotation of Daily Cash Recapitulation Sheets.

Month	Expla-nation	Cash sales gross	Total disburse-ments	Total purchases	Wages 104*	Supplies 402*	Rent 406*	Etc.
Jan								
Feb								
March								
April								
May								
June								
July								
Aug								
Sept								
Oct								
Nov								
Dec								
Total								

*These are ledger numbers of accounts; columns are made for all ledger accounts.

Totals are transferred to an annual summary, from which are prepared annual income statements and tax returns.

The only additional necessary financial records are accounts receivable, employee records, and fixed assets for depreciation purposes.

The daily records from which these figures have been taken may be punched and filed in a ring binder, with all supporting papers, such as receipts, cash register tapes, duplicates of deposit slips.

Fig. 11-3. Monthly Summary—Cumulative One-Book Summary of Daily Records.

General ledger

No matter what system you use—whether one or several journals or a daily cash recapitulation system—the information you will need is accumulated from the same sources and in the same categories:

1. assets
2. liabilities
3. income
4. expenses
5. net worth

The general ledger contains all necessary figures for a financial statement. It records and classifies all economic activities of the business.

The general ledger has one page for each record. All pages are numbered. There may also be one page for each customer who has a charge account. Here are some suggested pages and typical numbering:

Assets
101 cash
102 petty cash
103 accounts receivable
104 inventory
105 supplies
106 equipment
107 real estate
108 accumulated depreciation

Liabilities
201 accounts payable
202 notes payable

Income
301 sales
302 sales returns and allowances
303 other income

Expenses
401 rent
402 wages
403 utilities
404 advertising
405 repairs
406 maintenance
407 insurance
408 professional fees
409 travel
410 payroll taxes
411 donations
412 interest
413 sales tax
414 federal income taxes
415 other taxes
416 cash over and short
417 inventory
418 depreciation

Capital Accounts
501 capital
502 owner's drawer
503 profit

Taxes

601 federal withholding tax
602 FICA
603 state withholding tax
604 federal unemployment tax
605 state unemployment tax
606 county tax
607 federal income tax
608 state income tax
609 excise tax

Explanation of general ledger

101 checking account
102 money in cash drawer and in petty cash
103 accounts receivable if you carry charge accounts
104 physical count of inventory; for a business that does some of its own manufacturing there are three accounts—raw materials, goods in process, finished goods.
105 office supplies, wrapping supplies, etc.
106 cars, trucks, office equipment, cash registers, computers, etc. This is a fixed-asset account; there is a decrease in value because of charging off depreciation expense. This could be an accumulated depreciation account. When you debit depreciation expense, you credit accumulated depreciation as balancing entry.
107 If you own land and/or building on it, you will need a fixed-asset account and corresponding accumulated-depreciation account. There is depreciation on building but not on land.
108 accumulated depreciation; entry depends upon how accounts 106 and 107 are handled.
201 the bills you owe, particularly to vendors and suppliers.
202 When you borrow money, you credit this account for the amount borrowed and debit cash. You credit cash for the amount of the interest and debit the interest expense.
301 For trade discounts, enter net amount paid after taking discounts as actual purchase expenses.
302 sales returns and allowances
303 other income
400 For all operating expenses (all 400 accounts), whenever you pay an expense, you credit cash and debit expense account.
408 fees to attorneys, accountants, marketing research agencies, etc.
410 Social Security and withholding taxes withheld from salaries are owed by you to IRS; you debit salary expenses for the amount and credit this account; when you pay it to IRS you debit this account and credit cash. You match the Social Security amount with your tax payment. You also debit unemployment tax and credit cash.

413 Sales tax is collected when making a sale; it is recorded on the sales tickets or you use an approved formula to compute taxes on a day's sales. The amount collected is credited to this account and debited to cash. If your state allows a collection service discount, only the amount paid to the state is entered as a credit to cash; the discount allowed is credited to discounts earned (account 303).

416 You get this figure from your cash drawer reconciliation sheet.

418 Depreciation—this is different from when you deduct the portion of the cost each year; under this system you simply divide the cost by years of anticipated life to get annual depreciation expense; you debit depreciation expense and credit accumulated depreciation (account 108).

501 Capital—when you start a business, you invest cash and perhaps some assets; you credit this account and debit cash or other asset accounts in which the contribution was made. This account is also known as "owner's equity."

502 Whenever the owner draws out money, the cash is decreased; you debit this account and credit cash. The draw decreases owner's equity, so when the books are closed this account is credited and capital is credited.

503 Profit—owner's equity grows with profit; enter profit as debit to this account and credit capital (account 501). If you have a loss, the opposite set of entries is used.

600 This category is for the recording of all taxes and license fees.

Record books for the small store

A simple but adequate set of books for a small retail business includes a ledger, sales journal, check register, and an employee register if there are two or more employees.

A record should also be kept of all equipment acquisitions: acquisition date, cost, and depreciation. For such a system the journal will have many columns:

1. date
2. item and its description
3. check number
4. about twenty-four columns (rent, wages, advertising, utilities, etc.)
5. general ledger columns for less frequently used accounts

Sales journal

The sales journal includes daily recordings of all sales activities; they are figures taken from sales slips and cash register readings of all cash sales and cash for merchandise returned by customers. A modern cash register classifies sales and expenses, and provides daily subtotals and totals on cash register tapes. The sales journal also includes layaway transactions, charge account sales and returns, sales returns charged on credit cards other than those of the store, for example, Visa, American Express, MasterCharge.

Accounts payable journal

An accounts payable journal may be practical for a retail business where accounts payable are mostly to vendors of merchandise. A separate page is used for each vendor, listing name and address of vendor, amount of purchase, discount data, and each payment's date, amount, and check number. See Fig. 11-4.

Accounts receivable journal

An accounts receivable journal or a card file for each customer transaction is useful for the store that has many charge account or layaway customers. Information listed includes name and address of the customer, date and amount of the purchase, credits for returns of merchandise, and payments. The totals of the accounts receivable and payable journals are posted in the ledger. See Fig. 11-4.

Check register

In the check register or on the checkbook stubs are recorded all cash income and disbursements as money deposited or withdrawn. The checkbook should indicate check number, payee, purpose of payment, date, amount, and ledger page number. If the check is payment for merchandise, there should also be recorded the purchase order number and date. In the ledger under its appropriate category are posted the sales journal and check register entries. See Fig. 11-5.

Sales tickets

A sales ticket is prepared for all sales to customers; it is written in duplicate for cash sales, in triplicate for charge sales. The original is given to the customer; the duplicate and triplicate copies are for company files. These tickets are marked

Use a separate page for each vendor.

VENDOR _____ Address _____ Discount terms _____

Purchase Amt. Date due	Discount	Returns & credits	Due	Payment Amount Date	Check #	Balance

Use a separate page for each charge account and layaway customer.

CUSTOMER _____ Address _____ Charge _____ Layaway _____

Purchase Amt. Date	Returns & credits	Carrying charge	Due	Payment Amt. Date	Balance due

Fig. 11-4. Accounts Payable Journal, Accounts Receivable Journal.

Compare cancelled checks with register and bank statement.

Reconcile bank statement with checkbook:

bank balance $ _____

plus deposits not recorded by bank $ _____

less outstanding checks $ _____ $ _____

bank balance should be same as checkbook balance $ _____

Keep and file all cancelled checks, duplicate deposit slips, vouchers, paid invoices.

Charge account sales tickets are kept for several years; cash sales slips are kept for one year.

Fig. 11-5. Reconciliation of Bank Account with Check Register.

''cash'' or ''charge'' or ''layaway.'' At the end of the day or the next morning, before the store is open for business, the cash register is cleared and the cash reconciliation form prepared, using this data.

For transactions made with credit cards other than those of this store, the credit card company provides forms that are filled out in triplicate for purchases and for credit for returned merchandise; one copy is given to the customer, one is mailed to the credit card company, and one is retained for the store's own files.

Keeping track of petty cash

At the very opening of a business, a check should be drawn for petty cash. This check should be cashed and the money put in a drawer or box. Money taken from this for postage, freight, coffee, and other such items is noted on a printed form (Figure 24), giving the purpose and date withdrawn and initials of the drawee. At the end of the month, totals are posted in the ledger on the page of its corresponding account number. See Fig. 11-6.

A word about taxes

The general ledger discussed earlier has a page devoted to taxes. These include:

Federal excise taxes

Federal excise taxes are made on the sale of certain items—beer, liquor, diesel fuel, certain motor oils, petroleum products, firearms, trucks, and other items. Contact the local IRS office if you think you may fit in such a category. Form 720 accompanies all such tax payments.

State taxes

State taxes vary, but all states have unemployment tax, and most have sales tax and income tax. The income tax imposed by many states is deducted from wages. In

Cash voucher   No. _____

Date _____

Pay to _____

Description	Amount	Account no.
_____	_____	_____
_____	_____	_____
_____	_____	_____

Approved by _____ Entered by _____

Receipt of above is acknowledged _____

Office fund voucher   No. _____

From _____ 19 __ to _____ 19 __

Date	Receipt no.	To whom paid	For what	Acct no.	Amt.	Paid by check no.
___	___	___	___	___	___	___

Total disbursed _____

Cash _____

Amount of fund $100

Distribution

Acct. no.	Acct. no.	Acct. no.
_____	_____	_____
_____	_____	_____
_____	_____	_____

Total _____

Fig. 11-6. Petty Cash Records.

some states, if you fail to pay sales tax that you collected, you can be charged with embezzlement.

Local taxes

Local taxes vary. If there is a business license fee, it is usually a tax. Information is available in the *Tax Guide for Small Businesses*, U.S. Treasury Department, Government Printing Office, Washington, District of Columbia.

See worksheet for tax payments in Fig. 11-7.

Kind of tax	Due date	Amount due	Pay to	Date for writing check
ANNUAL				
Federal				
income				
self employment				
unemployment				
withholding				
Social Security				
excise				
workers compensation				
State				
income				
unemployment				
sales				
others				
Local				
sales				
real estate				
personal property				
licenses				
other				
QUARTERLY				
Federal				
estimated income tax				
income tax withholding deposits				
other				
State				
estimated income tax				
withholding tax deposits				
sales tax				

Fig. 11-7. *Worksheet for Tax Payments.*

What the bookkeeper does and when

This is the daily routine:

1. Sales slips are collected.
2. Cash register is cleared.
3. Cash reconciliation form is filled out.
4. Deposit slip is made.
5. Money for day is put in cash register drawer.
6. Daily transaction entries are made on monthly summary sheet or in daily journal.

This is the weekly routine:

1. Weekly payroll records are made.
2. Wages are prepared.
3. Accounts receivable are reviewed and action taken on slow accounts.

This is the monthly routine:

1. Bank statement is reconciled.
2. Journal and check register entries are posted to ledger.
3. Petty cash record is posted to ledger; check is written for replenishment.
4. Invoices are checked against monthly statements from vendors; checks are written for accounts payable.
5. Ledger accounts are totaled.
6. Trial balance of ledger accounts is taken.

This is the monthly routine of owner-manager:

1. Returns to suppliers are made.
2. Inventory control is examined; slow-moving merchandise is reduced in price or removed as dead stock; fast-moving merchandise is checked for adequacy of stock.
3. Charge accounts are reviewed.
4. Financial statements prepared by bookkeeper are reviewed.

At the end of the month, the books are closed, and ledger figures are summarized on a worksheet. This worksheet is used to strike a trial balance and make necessary adjustments. The trial balance column data is the net total of each of the ledger accounts. Total debits must equal total credits of the worksheet. If they are not equal, you have made an error that needs correcting.

12

The science of accounting

A BOOKKEEPING SYSTEM OF WHATEVER FORM SHOULD PROVIDE THE BUSINESS with raw data for preparation of three control documents:

1. The balance sheet, which tabulates all assets and all debts.
2. The income statement, also known as the profit and loss statement, which is an earning statement that tabulates the income and operating expenses, and the resulting profit or loss for the period.
3. Cash flow, which is a financial statement that indicates the ability of the business to pay its current bills.

These three records are your budgetary tools and also your problem identifiers. They must be used consistently and correctly.

What is a balance sheet?

The balance sheet is an orderly list of the dollar value on a given day of all that your business owns—its assets, and what it owes—its liabilities, and the dollar difference between the two—the owner's equity. The balance sheet is a position statement; it reports the dollar value of assets and equities in the company. The financial position can be described at any point in terms of: the resources the business owns—the assets, and claims or interests of parties (creditors) in these resources—the equity. The balance sheet is prepared usually at the end of an accounting period, and is dated the last day of the fiscal period because it tells the financial position of the business on that day.

The figures on the balance sheet are the amount of value that flows through the business operation and the amount left as the result of operation. The company's money is cash, additional cash received from sales and other income sources, and money invested in inventory and equipment. All of these items are recorded as assets.

The company owes money for bills not yet paid, such as accounts payable for inventory. These are listed as liabilities, current and long-term. Also listed as liabilities are the owners' and others' money invested in the business.

When you buy equipment, you reduce your cash assets but increase your fixed assets; when you borrow money, you add to your assets but also increase your liability.

Your balance sheet compares what is owed (liabilities) with what is owned (assets), which include accounts receivable, inventory, fixtures, and money in the bank. The assets less liabilities equal net worth of the business. Assets less liabilities represent the profit owed to the owner. Profit and cash are not synonymous. Nor is net income synonymous with profit. Net income is revenues (sales) less expenses.

Working capital is surplus of *current* assets over *current* liabilities. The purpose of the balance sheet is to show whether the business can pay its debts and still have working capital. What is the liquidation value of the assets? These figures should be compared with the standard rates for like businesses. Its assets depict everything that has money value. Cash is the most liquid of your assets, but your assets also include accounts receivable, marketable securities, inventory— everything that can readily be turned into cash. If your marketable assets are equal to current liabilities, your firm is strong but you are lacking in cash.

A group of clients, three women who owned a religious book store, were disturbed that the figures at the end of the year indicated that their business had made a profit of $6,000, but they couldn't find the $6,000. It certainly was not in the bank. In fact, the cash on hand was barely enough to pay current bills. My assignment was to find the $6,000. I found it—tied up in non-cash assets, the inventory of a newly introduced jewelry department. The partners learned the hard way that cash and profit are not synonymous.

Preparing a balance sheet

In estimating the cost of going into business, when you list current and fixed assets you are preparing a budget, and you are preparing a part of the balance sheet, the assets. The liabilities and net worth of the business are the rest of the information reported on the balance sheet.

Look at sample balance sheets in Figs. 12-1 through 12-4. Assets include current assets and fixed assets, an itemization of the dollar value of all that the business owns. Under liabilities are the debts of the business, the dollars owed. Assets include cash and claims to cash, and assets that have been acquired for business use—inventory and equipment.

Opening Day

February 22, 1990

McCracken Bookstore

Assets

Current assets

cash on hand	8,000		
cash in reserve*	9,000		
merchandise inventory	30,000		
prepaid expenses	1,000		
total current assets		48,000	

Fixed assets

fixtures	6,000		
office furniture & equipment	2,000		
remodeling and decorating	2,000		
total fixed assets		10,000	
total assets			58,000

Liabilities

current liabilities**	18,000		
contracts payable	3,000		
total current liabilities		21,000	
fixed liabilities***	15,000		
total fixed liabilities		15,000	
total liabilities			36,000

Net worth

Elizabeth McCracken, proprietor

assets	58,000		
liabilities	−36,000		
total net worth		22,000	

Total liabilities plus net worth**** 58,000

----

* reserve to cover accounts due
** due to suppliers of furniture fixtures
*** notes payable 4-year loan
****total liabilities plus net worth (36,000 + 22,000)

Fig. 12-1. Balance Sheet of Sole Proprietorship.

Mark Paul Photographics

Assets			Liabilities		
current assets			current liabilities		
cash	2,300		accounts payable	2,000	
accounts receivable	3,200		note payable	1,000	
inventory	5,400		contracts payable	1,500	
prepaid expenses	600				
Current assets		11,500	Current liabilities		4,500
fixed assets			fixed liabilities		
equipment	7,000		contracts payable	2,500	
less depreciation	1,500		long-term note payable	1,000	
Total fixed assets		5,500	Total fixed liabilities		3,500
Total assets		17,000	Total liabilities		8,000

Net worth		
Paul Matulef, partner	6,000	
Mark Matulef, limited partner	3,000	
Net worth	9,000	
Net worth + liabilities		17,000

Assets (17,000) − liabilities (8,000) = net worth (9,000)

Net worth (9,000) + liabilities (8,000) = assets (17,000)

Fig. 12-2. Balance Sheet of Partnership.

The assets column total must always be the same as the net worth column total. Assets must always equal equities. The sum of all resources must be equal to the sum of the claims on these resources. The total claims against assets must always be equal to total assets.

The equity section of the balance sheet is sometimes labeled "liabilities and owner's equity." Both creditors and owners have equity in the business. To get the owner's equity—total net worth—subtract total liabilities from total assets. The owner's equity may be divided into the amount originally invested and money added from earnings. Assets less liabilities is the working capital.

There are two ways of writing balance sheets. In the report form, assets are listed first, with liabilities and equity listed below (see Figs. 12-1 and 12-3). When assets and liabilities are in two side-by-side columns, they are in the account form (see Figs. 12-2 and 12-4).

Also see Figs. 12-5 and 12-6 for advice on how to prepare and construct a balance sheet.

Matulef Art Supplies

June 5, 1990

Assets

current assets

cash	4,200	
accounts receivable	25,400	
inventory	38,020	
prepaid expenses	500	
total current assets		68,120

fixed assets

equipment	40,100	
building	30,000	
less reserve for depreciation	9,000	
total fixed assets		61,100
Total assets			129,220

Liabilities

current liabilities

accounts payable	24,100	
Total current liabilities		24,100

long-term liabilities

mortgage payable	10,000	
total long-term liabilities		10,100
Total liabilities			34,200

Net worth*

preferred stock	15,000	
common stock	65,000	
retained earnings	15,020	
total net worth**		95,020
Total liabilities plus net worth		129,220

---

*also known as equity
**assets—liabilities, also known as working capital

Fig. 12-3. Balance Sheet of Corporation.

Balance Sheet

Jacobsons

January 2, 1990

Assets		Liabilities	
Current assets		Current liabilities	
(1) cash	1,000	(9) accounts payable	1,400
(2) accounts receivable	2,500	(10) accrued expenses	750
(3) inventory	2,000	(11) short-term loan	1,000
(4) Other current assets	500		
Total current assets	6,000	Total current liabilities	3,150
Fixed assets		Long-term liabilities	
(5) land	3,000	(12) bank loan payable	5,000
(6) building	15,000	(13) mortgage	7,000
(7) equipment	2,500	total long-term liabilities	12,000
(8) other fixed assets	5,500	Total liabilities	15,150
Total fixed assets	26,000	Owner's equity	16,850
Total assets	32,000	Owner's equity + liabilities	32,000

Explanation

(2) money owed by customers

(3) stock of merchandise

(7) furniture, fixtures, machinery

(8) anything else owned that can generate cash

(9) owed to vendors and other suppliers

(10) Owed for salaries, utilities, insurance, taxes, interest, mortgage

Owner's equity is his investment plus profit

Net worth (capital) is difference between total assets and total liabilities.

Fig. 12-4. Account Style of Balance Sheet.

ASSETS

Current assets

1. Cash

   This is a total of the cash in the bank, the store's cash registers, and the petty cash drawer.

2. Inventory

   This is the name for the saleable merchandise.

3. Accounts receivable

   Listed only. Businesses that sell on credit. Allowance is made for uncollectible accounts.

4. Other current assets

5. Total current assets

Fixed assets

6. Furniture

7. Fixtures

8. Equipment

9. Depreciation

   Depreciation, sometimes listed as Reserve for Depreciation, is a way of saving money over a designated period of years for specified equipment replacement. It is not actually a cash fund. Fixed assets wear out or become obsolete, and must be replaced. A part of their cost is written off as depreciation expense each fiscal period. Depreciation value is cost less salvage value. The most widely used book-keeping procedure for small businesses is to provide for an equal depreciated deduction in each year of the life of the item. Different types of fixed assets have different lengths of usefulness. Machinery is depreciated over a period of 5 to 10 years; store equipment, 2 to 10 years. Land is not depreciated. The buildings on the land are depreciated over a period of about 20 years. No firm can charge off more depreciation than the cost of the asset. Each fixed asset should have its own account in the financial records. Depreciation appears on the balance sheet as deductions from cost value of fixed assets; on income statements, as expenses.

10. Other fixed assets

11. Total fixed assets

12. Total assets

LIABILITIES

Current liabilities

13. Accounts payable

   These in a retail store are largely for merchandise; payment is usually due within 30 to 60 days, depending upon credit terms.

Fig. 12-5. How to Prepare a Balance Sheet.

14. Short-term notes

Usually a bank loan to pay for inventory, and requiring no collateral as guarantee of payment

15. Other current liabilities

These could be for rent, wages, interest, reserve for federal taxes based monthly estimate.

16. Total current liabilities

Fixed liabilities

17. Long-term notes payable

Obligation to pay over a period of years, e.g., mortgages, long-term loans, contracts

18. Other fixed liabilities

19. Total fixed liabilities

20. Total liabilities

NET WORTH

21. Retained earnings

Accumulation of profits not withdrawn by owners or distributed as cash dividends, for purpose of long-range planning for growth.

22. Net worth

Net worth of the proprietor is investment provided for starting the business plus profits less amount withdrawn by the owner. Net worth is calculated by subtracting total liabilities from total assets.

23. Total liabilities plus net worth

This figure must be the same as that recorded as total assets. Assets less liabilities equals owner's equity; this figure is also known as capital or working capital. The amount of working capital indicates ability of the business to meet bills as they come due.

Capital, or owner's equity, plus total liabilities, indicates that theoretically the creditors own part of the business because they helped to finance it when they extended credit.

BALANCE SHEET

Name

Date

ASSETS

Current Assets

    1. Cash

    2. Inventory

Fig. 12-5. Continued.

    3. Accounts receivable
    4. Other current assets
        5. Total current assets

Fixed Assets

    6. Furniture
    7. Fixtures
    8. Equipment
    9. Depreciation
    10. Other fixed assets
        11. Total fixed assets

12. Total assets

LIABILITIES

Current liabilities

    13. Accounts payable
    14. Short-term note payable
    15. Other current liabilities
        16. Total current liabilities

Fixed liabilities

    17. Long-term note payable
    18. Other fixed liabilities
        19. Total fixed liabilities

20. Total liabilities

NET WORTH*

    21. Retained earnings
    22. Net worth

23. Total liabilities and net worth

*Stockholders' equity
 Capital stock
 Retained stock
 Total liabilities and stockholders' equity

Fig. 12-5. Continued.

Current assets include:

cash

marketable securities

government securities

notes receivable

accounts receivable

inventory (unsold goods)

prepaid expenses

other items convertible to cash within one year

Fixed assets include:

land

buildings

equipment

leasehold improvements

items that have expected business life measured in years

Other assets include:

intangibles such as patents, royalty arrangements, copyrights

notes received from officers and employees

Current liabilities include:

accounts payable

notes payable

accrued expenses

wages and salaries

taxes payable

current portion of long-term debt

other obligations coming due within month

Long-term liabilities include:

mortgages

trust deeds

intermediate and long-term bank loans

other loans

equipment loans

any extraordinary items, e.g., pending lawsuits

Fig. 12-6. How to Construct a Balance Sheet.

13

The income statement and calculating profit

THE BALANCE SHEET ALONE DOES NOT PRESENT THE TRUE VALUE OF YOUR business. It gives a static picture of the business at a given *point in time*, for example, December 31, 1989. The income statement shows all of the income during a specified *period of time*, for example, January 1, 1989 to December 31, 1989, and all of the expenses incurred during that same period. The income statement is also called the "profit and loss statement." Still another name for it is "operating statement"; its figures provide data for analysis of sales. For an established business, it is the previous year's earning statement. For a new business it is a projection, an estimate of what earnings will be. See income statements in Figs. 13-1 and 13-2.

Income projections are income statements cast into the future—"estimate of income and expenses." You don't need a crystal ball; you need not be 100 percent accurate, but these projections help set short-term goals and budgets.

In a start-up situation, use income ratios for similar businesses. (See Chapter 15 for a description of ratios.) Most expenses are predictable, and income does not fluctuate drastically. However, some expenses cannot be foreseen, so be conservative in your estimates: underestimate sales and overstate expected expenses. Review and revise projections as you go along, to detect deviations as soon as possible. Be honest—this financial statement is for your own use.

In the bookkeeping process, at the end of the fiscal year the income statement is prepared as a summary of income and expenses. If total income exceeds total expenses, the company has made a profit. If expenses exceed income, the company has experienced a loss. The resulting profit or loss record is transferred to the owner's net worth account.

Cash is not necessarily profit. You can have considerable cash but owe

CASH RECEIPTS

1. Income from sales	$109,000		
2. Other income			
3. Gross sales	109,000		
4. Less returns, allowances, sales tax	−3,000		
Net sales (gross income)		106,000	

COST OF GOODS SOLD

5. Inventory at beginning of year	24,000		
6. Purchases during year	+ 72,000		
7. Inventory at end of year	− 25,000		
8. Cost of goods sold		71,000	
Gross profit			35,000

OPERATING EXPENSES

9. Salaries	14,000		
10. Rent	3,000		
11. Interest on loans	70		
12. Taxes, licenses	1,900		
13. Bad debts	250		
14. Repairs	235		
15. Depreciation	2,000		
16. Supplies	800		
17. Advertising	3,200		
18. Utilities	1,900		
19. Insurance	500		
20. Other operating expenses	400		
Total operating expenses		28,255	
Net profit before taxes			6,745

---

*also, projected profit and loss statement form

*Fig. 13-1. Income Statement.**

money. You can be short on cash but rich in accounts receivable. Cash does not always come in immediately upon making a sale, nor do you pay for your inventory immediately upon its arrival—it may take thirty, sixty, or even ninety days. In a toy shop, Christmas merchandise may be shipped to you in July or August; spring fashion apparel may reach your store in December.

Year ending December 31

1985 1986 1987 1988 1989

Income

Deductions

Expenses

Interest

Income tax

Income before
  extraordinary items

Net income

Retained earnings at
  beginning of period

This form gives you a picture of your business for a period of five years—a thumbnail analysis but an important one.

Fig. 13-2. Comparative Income Statement.

Ratios have been developed by statisticians to indicate the relationship of the items on the income statement with those on the balance sheet, and the relationship of the figures of this year with those of previous years, and those of businesses similar to yours. Chapter 15 is devoted to this analysis.

Such historical records tell you whether you are improving, declining, or standing still. They help you set up a budget for the following year, and most important of all, they tell you if you have money enough to pay this month's bills.

How to make an income statement
Cash receipts

1. Income from Sales. Money received in payment for products sold or services rendered; deposits in that amount were made to the store's bank account. Sales made on credit are not recorded until they are paid for; they are recorded on the balance sheet as accounts receivable as part of the assets.

2. Other Income. Money received from sources other than sales or services.

3. Gross Sales. Total of 1. and 2. This is also known as gross income.

4. Less Returns, Allowances, Sales Tax. Returns by customers and other such adjustments.

Net Sales (Gross Income). The retail price paid for merchandise sold; it is sometimes called revenue, but it is not income.

Cost of goods sold

Various deductions are made from gross sales, for example, cost of goods sold, operating expenses. In the first month of a new business, the cost of the full inventory is recorded; in the second month, what was left over from month number one after deducting sales and adding new deliveries. Cost of goods sold is:

5. Inventory. Inventory at beginning of year, plus.

6. Purchases. Purchases during year, minus.

7. Inventory. Inventory at end of year, to get.

8. Cost. Cost of goods sold.

Cost of goods sold is the total cost of the product; in a company that manufactures the products it sells, for example, a baker, the material is sometimes called "direct material" and the labor is called "direct labor." The total cost of the product is the sum of direct material, direct labor, and overhead, which is expense specifically related to direct material and direct labor.

Gross profit is gross income (net sales) less cost of goods sold.

Operating expenses

9. Salaries. Salaries include employees' take-home pay plus cost to the business of employees, such as Social Security, group health insurance, and unemployment taxes. The owner's salary is also included.

10. Rent. Rent is paid in advance.

11. Interest. Only the interest shows up on this statement; the principal is not "used up"—it is only borrowed for a while and then given back.

12. Taxes and Fees. Taxes, licenses.

13. Bad Debts. Bad debts include uncollectible accounts, bad checks.

These expenses are tabulated and totalled (20). You will learn later why expenses are not all thrown into one pot in bookkeeping tabulations.

14-20. Operation Expenses. Operation expenses.

21. Total Operating Expenses. Total operating expenses.

22. Net Profit Before Taxes. Net sales less total of cost of goods sold (8) plus total operating expenses (21) equal net profit before taxes (22). Net profit may consist of cash, accounts receivable (for merchandise sold to customers on credit and not yet paid for), and income from other sources, such as interest on investments. Salable but unsold merchandise is also profit. Dividends on corporation reports are shares in net income.

Taxes are neither profit nor loss; they are the government's share of the earnings. To calculate taxes, you add profits for the taxable year, subtract losses and other deductibles; if the result is a profit, you pay a percentage of the amount. Income regulations change from time to time. Get a copy of the IRS *Tax Guide for Small Business* to get the most recent information.

Profit: The business goal

You need a profit: That is what business is all about. If expenditures are balanced by the same amount of income dollars you have no profit, no loss. You are breaking even—no hits, no runs.....no errors? Well, maybe no errors in baseball language, but in business there is an error somewhere, perhaps even a disaster. Your income must be greater than your expenditures. You need a profit to stay in business, and you need a return on your investment.

Start out by deciding realistically how much profit you want to make, and what you expect to be able to make. See profit anticipation Fig. 13-3.

Investing in a business is for the purpose of increasing the size of investment in that business. The word for that is PROFIT. If it costs you more money to operate the business than the income you will receive, you are losing, not making, money. It's that simple. Also, if the percentage of profit you are making on your investment is less than the salary you could earn on a job plus the interest you could get from investing your money elsewhere, you are losing money.

To stay in business profitably you must receive a return on your cash investment; you must also receive a return on your time in terms of dollars. This is only reasonable.

This storekeeper wants to make a net profit of $10,000. His expenses are $5,000. His merchandise cost is 60% of his selling price. This is how he figures what his sales must be:

Net profit equals gross profit less expenses

$10,000 equals 0.4 times sales less $5,000

$10,000 plus $5,000 equals 0.4 times sales

$$\frac{15,000}{0.4} = \text{sales}$$

$$\text{sales} = \$37,500$$

He will need sales of $37,500 to make a net profit of $10,000.

EXPENSES

Amounts to be spent on expenses are expressed in averages; ordinarily should not exceed 23%.

rent	4%
salaries	8%
advertising	1%
bad debts	1%
delivery	2%
depreciation	1%
supplies	1%
miscellaneous	5%

Fig. 13-3. Profit Anticipation.

	Total	Fixed	Variable
Cost of goods sold	71,641		71,641
Salaries and wages	14,350	8,200	6,150
Rent	3,500	3,000	500
Interest	871	871	
Delivery	1,988		1,988
Bad debts	250	250	
Repairs	235	185	50
Depreciation	2,083	2,083	
Supplies and materials	860		860
Advertising	860	60	800
Utilities	2,100		2,100
Other operating expenses	891	591	300
Total expenses and costs	99,629	15,240	84,389

Use your judgment in the allocation. Salaries reflect extra help during busy seasons. A part of the rent reflects situations in which a percent of the gross becomes part of the rent.

Fig. 13-4. *Dividing Expenses Into Fixed and Variable.*

For business opening June 1

Month	Estimated sales	Cost of sales 35% markup	Gross profit	Fixed expenses	Variable expenses taxes	Net profit before
June	4,800	3,120	1,680	2,000	720	(−1,040)
July	7,200	4,680	2,520	2,000	1,080	(−560)
Aug	8,640	5,616	3,024	2,000	1,295	(−271)
Sept	9,600	6,240	3,360	2,000	1,440	(−80)
Oct	16,000	10,400	5,600	2,000	2,400	(1,200)
Nov	22,300	14,560	7,840	2,000	3,360	(2,480)
Dec	35,200	22,880	12,320	2,000	5,280	(5,040)
Jan	9,600	6,240	3,360	2,000	1,440	(−80)
Feb	9,600	6,240	3,360	2,000	1,440	(−80)
Mar	9,600	6,240	3,360	2,000	1,440	(−80)
Apr	9,600	6,240	3,360	2,000	1,440	(−80
May	9,600	6,240	3,360	2,000	1,440	(−80)

Note: Do not be dismayed if net profit some months is a minus figure; the figure to consider is the total for the year, coupled with cash flow projection.

Fig. 13-5. *Table of Net Profit Before Taxes.*

Whatever the reason you give for going into business, your object is, or should be, to make money. Your goal, you may have to remind yourself, is not to just go into business, but to stay in business for some time. And looking farther down the road, to be able to sell it at a profit whenever you want to withdraw.

Dividing expenses into fixed and variables

To estimate expenditures for operation of a business, there are fixed and variable expenses. Fixed expenses never vary; they are costs that remain constant despite sales volume, and even when you make no sales at all—rent, office expense, insurance, taxes, and depreciation. Fixed expenses can be estimated fairly accurately. Space charges are primarily rent and utilities; they must be paid on a monthly basis whether there is income from sales or not. Fixed payroll is the payroll expense for the minimum number of employees needed. It should include the owner at the employees' hourly rate. If the owner is a salesperson as well as a manager, his salary should be included in operating expenses. For additional compensation for being the owner and having invested in the business, an additional amount is drawn as profit.

For business opening June 1

Month	% of annual sales	Normal	Adjusted for start-up	Adjusted monthly sales
June	6%	9,600	50%*	4,800
July	6%	9,600	75%**	7,200
Aug	6%	9,600	90%***	8,640
Sept	6%	9,600	100%	9,600
Oct	10%	16,000	100%	16,000
Nov	14%	22,400	100%	22,400
Dec	22%	35,200	100%	35,200
Jan	6%	9,600	100%	9,600
Feb	6%	9,600	100%	9,600
Mar	6%	9,600	100%	9,600
April	6%	9,600	100%	9,600
May	6%	9,600	100%	9,600

Estimated income for a new business:

*first month—50% of estimated income
**second month—75% of estimated income
***third month—90% of estimated income

Fig. 13-6. Table of Monthly Sales Projection.

Variable expenses include merchandise, which is figured at cost (sixty percent is the average figure), and this covers transportation and losses due to breakage, spoilage, theft, mark downs; it also takes into account suppliers' discounts and costs associated with sales—commissions to salespersons, delivery, variable labor costs, management-controlled expenses such as advertising, supplies, plus a percentage for unidentified expenses.

See Fig. 13-4 for dividing fixed and variable expenses. Figure 13-5 presents a table of net profit before taxes, and Fig. 13-6 presents monthly sales projections.

14

Cash flow, forecasting and budgeting

THE CASH FLOW STATEMENT IS THE THIRD IMPORTANT FINANCIAL DOCUMENT, and probably the single most important document for small business management. Cash flow is deposits in the bank minus checks that were written—total receipts less total disbursements. This is your net cash. This statement tells the cash available at a specific time to pay specific bills that are due; it tells exactly how much money is available to meet immediate obligations. Cash is the fuel that runs the business. Cash flows out to pay for merchandise and the operating expenses. Cash inflow must be equal to or greater than cash outflow.

Cash flow is only when somebody pays for something. It is not the same as profit. It comes from sales, but not all sales are cash sales. Keep in mind that cash flow deals only with cash transactions.

Cash flow is the most critical planning tool. Cash flow statements show how much cash will be needed, when it will be needed, and where it will come from. There need be no unexpected borrowing. With this statement as your guide, when you borrow it will be for a specific amount at a specific time, which will keep interest payments down. If there is a surplus of cash, you may have borrowed too much.

Negative cash means that in your forecasting you will be going into the red to pay your bills. Negative cash flow in some months is normal, as has been indicated in the Table of Monthly Sales, Fig. 13-6. However, there are some instances when monthly sales figures indicate necessary action—reducing inventories, cutting expenses, applying for a bank loan or line of credit.

The cash flow statement shows how well cash is being managed—your liquidity. If expenses for given items increase over the budgeted amount, you can find out why and take corrective measures. If expenses are lower than anticipated, this may indicate that some of your bills have been overlooked or that there is another problem. Cash flow is also your budget statement.

Your prospects will indicate your ability to repay loans or other fixed debts. A cash flow statement may be required by a lender, who will want to know how fast you can repay a loan; he will want to know the estimated cash flow for the next three months or the next year.

The balance sheet and income statement will tell you where you have been. Cash flow, a profit forecast, tells you where you are going. As a forecasting device, it's the way to evaluate future bank balances by showing when cash comes in and when it's paid out. Businesses with good sales and good profit can fail because of lack of cash when bills are due. Stores that carry their own charge accounts must be particularly aware of this in their collection methods. Sending out statements several days before the end of the month may help to bring in cash by the first of the month, when many of your own bills come due.

Timing of cash flow is important in determining the particular working capital requirements of the business. It is necessary to identify seasonal characteristics. For example, in a midwest garden shop, you know your inventory peak will be in May; in a toy store, whatever its location, the peak will be in December. You will know the date and amount of financing you'll require. You *can* manage the future with this paper tool as your profit forecaster—cash flow. See cash flow and budget Figs. 14-1 through 14-5.

Preparing a cash flow statement

A cash flow statement is prepared like a checkbook reconciliation. It would read like this.

Cash balance at beginning of month	$4,280
Cash receipts (plus)	3,550
Cash disbursements (minus)	2,500
Cash balance at end of month	5,330

Details of above:

1. cash in register, petty cash drawer, bank
2. received from current month sales, collections on accounts receivable, other anticipated income
3. new inventory purchases, new equipment purchases, salaries, rent, utilities, insurance, advertising, maintenance, miscellaneous
4. item 1. plus 2. minus 3.
5. item 4. above

	Jan	Feb	Mar	Apr	May	June
Receipts						
sales						
collections						
other						
Total						
Disbursements						
rent						
salaries						
utilities						
inventory						
insurance						
advertising						
maintenance						
other						
Total						
Cash flow						
beginning balance						
ending balance						

INCOME STATEMENT FORECAST

	Jan	Feb	Mar	Apr	May	June
Revenue						
sales						
Expenses						
inventory						
cost of goods sold						
gross profit						
Disbursements						
rent						
salaries						
utilities						
others (as above)						
total expenses						
Pre-tax profit						
Taxes						
NET PROFIT						

Fig. 14-1. Cash Flow Forecast.

Retail Business

Month	A Cash inflow	B Cash outflow	C Cumulative cash inflow	D Cumulative cash outflow	E Cumulative difference
Jan	1,500	3,100	1,500	3,100	(1,600)
Feb	2,500	3,800	4,000	6,900	(2,900)
March	3,500	4,500	7,500	11,400	(3,900)
April	3,500	4,500	11,000	15,900	(4,900)
May	3,500	4,500	14,500	20,400	(5,900)
June	5,500	6,000	20,000	26,400	(6,400)
July	5,000	5,600	25,000	32,000	(7,000)
Aug	4,500	5,200	29,500	37,200	(7,700)
Sept	4,000	4,900	33,500	42,100	(8,600)
Oct	6,000	6,300	39,500	48,400	(8,900)
Nov	19,000	15,700	58,500	64,100	(5,600)
Dec	41,500	31,900	100,000	96,000	(4,000)

C = A + C, previous month

D = B + D, previous month

E = A (+ or −) B (+ or −) E, previous month

Fig. 14-2. Seasonal Cash Flow.

Drawing up a budget

Profitable utilization of working capital requires careful planning—enough money to pay bills, enough for the owner's draw, enough set aside for future expansion. To operate a business requires all sorts of tools—housing, equipment, employees, insurance, light, heat, and advertising. Effectiveness of each of these operational items of expense determines the profit or loss, success or failure of the store.

Each item of expense on the budget statement is expressed as a percentage of sales. The major purpose of budgeting is expense control. It is wise to keep expenses in line with the available data of others in similar businesses, of like firms. Reporting agencies such as Dun and Bradstreet provide operating ratios and expense data, which give the entrepreneur a common base as he estimates how much money to allot to each expense item. Standard operating ratios for *Expenses in Retail Business*, published by National Cash Register Company, and *Barometer of Small Businesses*, published by Accounting Corporation of America, are excellent sources. Figure 15-3 provides a list of such sources of data for specific businesses.

The importance of each item listed as an expenditure, what it produces and what it costs, becomes a fixed percentage of total expenses as one prepares a projected income statement and budget. There is a minimum percentage that each item can cost and still be useful, and a maximum that it can cost before it reduces profit.

However, as important as these statistics are, expenses must relate to the goal that you've set for yourself. Standard percentages of industry must be modified for your kind of business. Is it a discount store, requiring low overhead? Is it an exclusive boutique, where price is set to absorb somewhat exaggerated expenses? Expenses must be appropriate to goals. One item balances another; high advertising may be balanced by low rent. At the end of the year, you learn whether you have made as much profit as you should have made, or whether your expenses were too high; you judge this by studying the detailed figures, item by item.

It is important to include imputed as well as actual costs in the expense account. Actual expenses are utilities, rent, labor, and interest on loans. Imputed

April 1 to June 30, 19___

Budget   Actual

Anticipated cash receipts

cash sales

collections on cash receivables

other income

Total Cash Receipts

Anticipated cash expenditures

payroll

merchandise

advertising

taxes

rent

utilities

others

Total cash expenditures

1. Anticipated cash balance at beginning of month ____

2. Cash increase less decrease (receipts less expenditures) ____

3. Anticipated cash balance at end of month (2. plus 1.) ____

4. Anticipated working cash balance ____

Fig. 14-3. Cash Budget Form.

To compare your results with your budget, have your accountant help you set up a deviation analysis. It is simple to maintain, and it is a valuable source of current information. It serves as a direct and quick control of your business. It tells you at a glance where your business is heading toward problems and where it is flourishing—what you are doing wrong, what you are doing right. It can help you to minimize expenses and increase profits.

Monthly Deviation Analysis

	Actual A	Budget B	Deviation C B − A
revenues			
less cost of goods sold			
gross margin			
expenses			
salaries			
rent			
utilities			
and others			
total cash expenditures			
income before taxes			
taxes			
Net profit			

Fig. 14-4. Monthly Cash Flow Deviation Analysis.

expenses are those that would be charged for property or services of the proprietor if they were secured from someone else. They include interest on capital invested by the proprietor, rent from the property he owns, and a fair salary. This is important to consider when you operate your business from your home, when a spouse does the bookkeeping without salary, when you use personal equipment.

With accurate, complete records of expense items, you will be able to tell whether expenses of each line item are too high or too low. Expense control means management control; if something is too expensive, do something about it. Higher-than-standard ratios in expenses generally indicates the need for expense reduction.

	Actual A	Budget B	Deviation C B − A
receipts			
beginning cash balance			
plus cash sales			
operating expenses			
inventory			
advertising			
rent			
salaries			
and other operating expenses			
total disbursements			
Ending cash balance			

Fig. 14-5. Monthly Cash Flow Deviation Analysis.

Preparing a budget requires two main documents: an income statement and a cash flow statement. The income statement shows how much was earned, how it was spent, and whether you showed a profit or loss within a specified period. The cash flow statement summarizes sources of cash, how it was spent, and amount of cash on hand.

A budget should itemize everything. It is based on past income and spending, and on projections of future income and spending. A new business does not have previous records on which to base projections, so it must rely on the best estimates available from consultants, suppliers, trade journals, and those in the same business.

The only difference in preparing a budget for a new business and for an ongoing business is that a new business will be concerned with expansion. Be sure that you have enough funds so that you don't risk current business. Above all, guard your good credit rating.

15

Ratios as yardsticks

MONEY IN THE CASH DRAWER AT THE END OF THE BUSINESS DAY DOES NOT really tell you that you have made money, nor does an empty cash drawer at the end of the day tell you that you have lost money and the reason why. But you need a way of knowing whether profits are adequate for the investment you made in the business and whether you are safely solvent. There is a way, simple to follow, to find answers to your important questions. The system is called "ratios." Its data comes from your own records: your current balance sheet and income statement. And to find out how you are doing compared to those in like businesses, look to their balance sheets and income statements. You'll find these in annual publications such as Dun and Bradstreet's *Key Business Ratios*, and Robert Morris Associates' *Annual Statement Studies,* and articles in periodicals such as *Business Week, Forbes, Fortune*, all available in public libraries.

See industry averages for retail stores and sources for average operating ratios in Figs. 15-1 and 15-2.

Ratios answer such questions as: What return am I getting on my investment? Am I overstocked? Understocked? Am I spending too much money on advertising? Not enough? Are my expenses excessive? How am I doing compared to last year? How does my operation compare to other businesses like mine?

Ratios provide a mathematical expression of a relationship, usually a percentage. Formidable at first and even at second glance, they are simple to create. You have all the necessary materials in your own records.

For example, to answer your question, "How much profit have I made this year?" use the ratio that indicates the relationship of profit to sales. Your profit was $8,000 and your sales were $160,000. You divide your profit by your sales; the answer is five percent.

$$\frac{\text{profit}}{\text{sales}} \qquad \frac{\$\ 8,000}{\$160,000} = 0.05$$

Your income is five percent of sales. For every one dollar of sales you had an income of five cents.

The list of ratios is endless, but you'll want to use only those that fit your particular information needs. As you study statistics of other businesses, you'll look to those of like businesses in your own area.

And you will use your own judgment in analyzing them. Ratios are an important financial tool, but you must exercise caution in their use. Never use a single ratio. Also, in studying "typical ratios," the established averages, be sure they are of stores similar to yours in size and location. And as important as ratios are as analytical tools, they are guides and not specific plans for action. There is no substitute for managerial judgment—your own understanding of your own business.

Ratios to determine solvency

The balance sheet of a business shows assets and liabilities, and net worth on a specific date. It separates current items, those to be paid or collected within the year, from fixed or long-term items that are to be paid or collected in a period of

Net profit to net worth	18.4%
Net profit to net sales	3.1%
Net sales to fixed assets	5.8%
Net sales to net worth	7.5%
Current ratio	1.3%
Acid test	1.0%
Accounts receivable to working capital	0.4%
Inventory to working capital	0.4%
Accounts receivable to average daily credit sales	430 days
Net sales to inventory	22.0%
Net sales to working capital	10.0%
Long-term liabilities to working capital	0.7%
Total liabilities to net worth	1.6%
Current liabilities to owner's equity	1.1%
Fixed assets to owner's equity (net worth)	1.2%

Fig. 15-1. Industry Averages for Retail Stores.

Automobile Retailing

National Automobile Dealers Assn., 2000 M Street, NW, Washington, D.C. 20006

Beauty Shops

Modern Beauty Shop, 59 E. Monroe, Chicago, Ill. 60603 *Beauty Shop Facts and Figures*

Book Stores

American Booksellers Assn., 175 Fifth Ave., New York, N.Y. 10010

Department and Specialty Stores

Retail Merchants Assn., 100 W. 31st St., New York, N.Y. 10010

Drugstores

Eli Lilly and Co., Indianapolis, Ind. 46225 *Annual Lilly Digest*

Furniture Stores

National Retail Furniture Assn., 66 Lake Shore Drive, Chicago, Ill. 60611

Hardware Stores

Retail Hardware Assn., 964 Pennsylvania Ave., Indianapolis, Ind. 46284 *Management Report*

Men's Wear

Men's Wear Magazine, 7 E. 12th Street, New York, N.Y. 10003 *Annual Survey*

Paint, Glass, Wallpaper Stores

Retail Paint and Wallpaper Distributors of America, 8131 Delmar Ave., St. Louis, Mo. 63130

Sporting Goods Stores

National Sporting Goods Assn., 23 E. Jackson Blvd., Chicago, Ill. 60604

Stationery Stores

National Stationery and Office Equipment Assn., 740 Investment Bldg., Washington, D.C. 20006 *Operating Results*

Toy Dealers

Playthings, 71 W. 23rd Street, New York, N.Y. 10010 *Operating Profits*

Fig. 15-2. Sources for Average Operating Ratios.

more than one year, long-term assets and long-lived objects such as equipment. The difference between *current* assets and *current* liabilities is net working capital, the money available for paying current bills.

A business is solvent, has liquidity, if it has cash when bills are due. Lack of liquidity can cause an otherwise solvent business to become insolvent. A business is insolvent when its current liabilities, its "due now" bills, exceed its current assets: it cannot pay its obligations even if all current assets are sold.

Current ratios

To know the ability of a store to meet its current debts, the most common ratio used is the current ratio, often called the "banker's rule of thumb." Figures are taken from the current balance sheet. Expressed as a percentage, current assets are divided by current liabilities.

$$\frac{\text{current assets}}{\text{current liabilities}}$$

That tells the number of dollars available to cover each dollar of current debts—the margin for protection of short-term creditors. For retail stores, for every dollar of debts there should be $2.50 in current assets, and it's advisable that the ratio not fall below 2:1. The higher the ratio, the more liquid the firm.

$$\begin{array}{cc} \text{current assets} & \\ \text{current liabilities} & \end{array} \qquad \frac{\$36{,}000}{\$14{,}000} = 2.57$$

There is $2.57 for every $1 of indebtedness. Let us take another example:

$$\begin{array}{cc} \text{current assets} & \\ \text{current liabilities} & \end{array} \qquad \frac{\$10{,}190}{\$12{,}500} = 0.81$$

There is 81¢ for every dollar owed.

This unhappy ratio of assets to liabilities indicates a cash shortage; it's an indication of poor management of working capital or undercapitalization of the store.

Obviously the most current asset is cash. Liquidity of assets is the ease with which other assets can be converted into cash. Looking at a balance sheet we see that current assets consist not only of cash but also of accounts receivable and inventory, items expected to be converted into cash quickly. The validity of these figures for analysis by ratio is determined by the actual value of these assets. Are the accounts receivable current? Is the merchandise salable at its marked price? In other words, how authentic are the asset figures? Added to the cash on hand, will income from merchandise sales the next few weeks be enough to pay all current bills coming due? Some current assets may be of doubtful value. Some accounts may be uncollectible. Seasonal fluctuations affect inventory value—high carryover from the previous season, or an inventory count at the end of a season, when stock is below its average size. This leads us to the conclusion that the current ratio is not 100 percent foolproof.

Acid test ratios

The acid test ratio answers the question of how fast the business can pay its bills. Quick assets consist only of items with a relatively stable dollar value, such as cash, marketable securities, and current accounts receivable. Inventory is not included in the assets. The industry average for retail stores is 1:0.

$$\frac{\text{current assets less inventory}}{\text{current liabilities}} \quad \frac{\$30,000}{\$14,000} = 2.14$$

Net working capital ratios

Working capital is the difference between current assets and current liabilities: the money left to pay for operation of the store.

total current assets	$35,355
less total current liabilities	$14,582
equals working capital	$20,773

Will $20,773 be sufficient operating capital for the coming period? Should there be an operating capital shortage, one source of the problem may be the amount invested in fixed assets. Too much money invested in fixed assets may leave too little for working capital. The solution for a company with substantial owner's equity, low on long-term debts and short of working capital, could be to finance current assets with a long-term loan.

$$\frac{\text{net sales}}{\text{working capital}} \quad \frac{\$168,000}{\$\,35,000} = 5x$$

Net sales to working capital ratios shows how many dollars of sales the company makes for every dollar it has of working capital.

Inventory turnover

This evaluation is useful in pointing out possible trouble ahead because of over-stocking or overevaluation of the worth of merchandise stock. "Inventory turn-over" is the number of times a year merchandise must be replenished. The retail industry average is five times. Inventories are usually valued at cost, but where it's more convenient to evaluate it at retail price, sales and receipts must also be measured at retail.

Normally a high turnover rate means salable inventory. Slow turnover may mean too much inventory for the sales capacity of the business: It suggests over-buying or the accumulation of unsalable goods. High turnover, although desirable usually, should not be taken at face value because it could be the result of inadequate inventory levels. Inventory usually is taken at the end of the calendar year, when firms have the smallest inventory of the entire period. Excessively high turnover may indicate the store is stocking fast-moving items and sales are lost because the store is out of stock. Inventory that turns over too slowly is probably caused by shelves loaded with slow items and working capital that is tied up, resulting in loss of sales due to lack of fresh merchandise. See Fig. 15-3 how to compute inventory turnover.

Profitability ratios

The figures for these ratios are taken from the profit and loss (income) statement. They relate to profit or sales: net profit equals sales less cost of goods sold and expenses.

$$\frac{\text{net profit before taxes}}{\text{net sales}} \qquad \frac{\$\ 4,286}{\$106,555} = 0.04$$

The profit from each one dollar of sales is four cents.

Net profit before taxes divided by net sales is the profit margin. It shows what part of every sales dollar is profit. The higher the percentage, the greater the efficiency of operation, and the greater the success of the management in keeping

Example:

cost of goods sold for year	$200,000 (see A below)
divided by average inventory at cost	$ 30,000 (see B below)
equals inventory turnover	6.6 times

Deduction from above: The company sells and replaces its inventory more than 6 times each year.

A

To get cost of goods sold for year:

cost of opening inventory	$ 35,000	
plus purchases during year	$194,000	
minus closing inventory	$ 29,000	
equals cost of goods sold		$200,000

B

To get average inventory:

inventory at beginning of year	$ 35,000	
plus inventory at end of year	$ 29,000	
equals	$ 64,000	
divided by 2 gives average inventory		$32,000

Fig. 15-3. How to Compute Inventory Turnover.

expenses under control. However, a low return can be practical, for example, for the store whose policy is low prices and large sales volume. Fixed costs do not rise in direct proportion to sales: for example, rent may stay the same.

$$\frac{\text{net profit}}{\text{total assets}} \quad \frac{\$\ 8,000}{\$45,000} = 0.18$$

This ratio tells the return on investment. It is the most important measure of the store's financial situation. Net profit is the return on investment, and return on investment should be related to all capital, whether it was supplied by the owner or by the lenders. It is a measure of money management. It is similar to net profit/ net worth, except that the latter takes into consideration only the owner's investment, as shown in the next ratio:

$$\frac{\text{net profit before taxes}}{\text{net worth}} \quad \frac{\$12,972}{\$99,030} = 0.13$$

This is known as a "mixed ratio" because it derives its figures from both the balance sheet and the income statement. It shows what yield or "interest rate" the investment in the business is bringing through profit. The rate of return always should be higher than the cost of borrowing money. The industry average for retail stores is thirty percent.

Efficiency ratios

Efficiency ratios, also known as "operating ratios," are used for expense control. The figures are taken from the income statement.

$$\frac{\text{current expenses}}{\text{sales (income)}} \quad \frac{\$\ 80,000}{\$100,000} = 0.80$$

It costs this company eighty cents to produce one dollar in sales. The store's profit is twenty cents of every dollar of sales. Operating expenses are classified as fixed and variable. Fixed costs cannot be changed appreciably, but variable costs can be controlled.

Higher-than-average operating expenses are not necessarily bad—look to the net profit ratio to see if that is satisfactory. It may reflect the store's policy to give better-than-average quality of merchandise and service. Nevertheless, a store with an expense ratio much higher than that of similar stores is likely to be unprofitable.

This ratio might be due to small sales volume as compared with that of a profitable store, and not necessarily to higher expenses, but it usually indicates low efficiency and poor management in controlling expenses.

Leverage ratios

Leverage ratios indicate the proportion of the business that belongs to the owner, and what proportion belongs to creditors. The higher the ratio the greater the risky position of the business. When these ratios are low the financial position is better, and the business has sufficient reserve assets to borrow on.

$$\frac{\text{total liabilities (debts)}}{\text{net worth (owners equity)}} \quad \frac{\$11,000}{\$20,000} = 0.56$$

This is a very important ratio. Debt capital is money provided by creditors; equity capital is money provided by the owner. Compare what is owed to what is owned as percentages approach 100 percent—as creditors' proportion approaches that of the owner. If it exceeds 100 percent the creditors own more than the owners, and the business is undercapitalized. In such a case, the owner should get a loan to increase his percentage of equity.

$$\frac{\text{total liabilities}}{\text{total assets}} \quad \frac{\$11,300}{\$31,300} = 0.36$$

This shows the percentage of assets provided by creditors. The higher the ratio, the more debt-heavy the assets. The more the creditors own, the less the "owner" owns; he has invested insufficient capital.

"Trading on the equity" refers to the relationship of credit (liabilities) to the owner's capital. "Trading on too-thin an equity" is the term used to describe those who have too little of their own money invested, as compared with creditor capital used to finance a business. Current liabilities should seldom be more than fifty percent of net worth. Proprietor ratio of fifty percent indicates that the owner has invested half the value of the total assets. When the ratio falls below fifty percent, further credit may be difficult to obtain.

Analyzing expenses
Rent

A rent ratio that is higher than that of similar businesses might be the result of the storeroom being larger than necessary to handle its present sales volume, or it could mean that the business's favorable location requires less advertising costs to attract customers. Low rent ratio may mean the retailer was able to get a good value—but remember, it's not a good value if the building is too small for the necessary sales volume; in such case the business owner should ask himself, "Can the location be improved by paying more rent?"

Advertising

Advertising expenses above the standard figure may represent increased sales and profit; however, if added sales consist mainly of staples or low-margin goods, advertising may not be profitable. If a percentage above standard advertising cost produces no greater percentage of sales than normal, the merchant must re-evaluate her advertising program. To be profitable, advertising must result in added-dollar gross margin more than sufficient to cover added-dollar advertising and other expenses. That is, advertising should sell goods carrying high gross margin rates as well as staples. If advertising expense ratio is below standard and is accompanied by small sales and net profits, it could indicate that one of the problems is insufficient advertising. Increased advertising may increase sales and profits.

Payroll

Keep payroll under control by employing the amount and kind of help you need to operate your store—more part-time employees willing to work when needed, such as former employees. Get qualified help; higher wages may pay off; take advantage of their special skills.

Supervise employees properly. A high employee-wage ratio may indicate too many clerks or inefficient use of staff. Low employee-wage ratio usually is evidence of efficient management, especially if accompanied by low total expense-of-operation ratio, and a satisfactory profit ratio. If sales are unsatisfactory, it may indicate that the store is not employing enough workers of the right kind. To determine the meaning of this ratio, however, you must study other ratios: sales volume, gross margin, expense.

Owner's draw

In studying net profit ratios, it's well to distinguish between the owner's salary and the owner's withdrawal of profits. Low wage ratio of owner and low net profit ratio indicate the owner is getting a small total return. Small withdrawal of profits by owner and satisfactory net profit indicate the retailer is building up his capital. Higher ratio may indicate the store earns large profits or that excessive wages are being paid to the owner.

Part IV

Structuring and funding the business

16

Insurable risks

A RETAIL BUSINESS FACES MANY RISKS—FIRE, FLOOD, BURGLARY, VIOLENT weather. You must have insurance, the most effective safeguard against losses resulting from such hazards. In buying insurance policies, you transfer the risk to someone else: the insurance company.

There's a limit to the precautions you can take to prevent potential disaster losses, but to be completely covered by insurance would require more than most businesses could afford. To determine what hazards warrant coverage by insurance, you must take into account your kind of business, its location, and the cost involved. The advice of a reliable, qualified insurance agent is the answer. Select him yourself; don't be selected by him.

Selecting an agent

You have the choice of using an insurance writer, or an independent agent or broker. A writer employed by an insurer is limited to the line of insurance carried by his employer. An independent agent represents several companies and types of insurance, and so he offers a wider choice of insurance companies than does a writer. A broker offers an even wider selection, and may be able to get you the best deal. There are agencies that specialize in certain types of insurance that are applicable to specific businesses; their cost may be somewhat lower.

In selecting an agent, look to his financial reputation and specialization in the type of coverage you require. If the broker or agent is a charter property and casualty underwriter—CPCU—you are guaranteed professionalism.

Using one agent or broker minimizes the chance of overlapping of policies. Overlapping inflates the cost and hinders settlement when a loss occurs.

Deciding which policies you need

As you consider in what areas you need insurance, many questions come to your mind.

What happens if a fire destroys the building or the entire stock of merchandise? While I am out of business because of this disaster, what is my responsibility to my employees?

What if I, the sole proprietor of the store, suddenly become seriously ill?

What if my bookkeeper, on the way to the bank in his own car to deposit the daily receipts, hits a pedestrian?

Accident

Highly polished floors

Wet or slippery or dark stairs

Stairs in unexpected places

Unanchored or torn rugs or other floor coverings

Projecting objects

Elevators and escalators unless regularly inspected

Aisles narrow or crowded

Merchandise on the floor

Entrance floormats that are not nonskid

Fire

Accumulation of waste paper and rags

Smoking in the store by customers or employees

Insufficient ashtrays if you permit smoking

Unmarked fire exits

Frayed electric wires

Fire extinguishers needing recharging

Ceiling lights too close to the ceiling

Electric light bulbs too close to the merchandise

No sprinkler system in store or stockroom

Exit doors that swing in

Furnaces not insulated

Fig. 16-1. Accident Hazards, Fire Hazards.

What if I find out that my clerk has been stealing merchandise?

What if a pair of pajamas bought in my store catches on fire from a cigarette spark while a child is wearing them?

See Fig. 16-1 for other potential accident and fire hazards.

It is concerns such as these that you'll face as you meet with your agent. Ask him to draw up a plan of recommended coverage and the estimated premiums, guided by the most economical plan that recognizes the risks to which your kind of business is exposed. A paint store has different risks than a children's clothing store. Buy only what you need, but don't be underinsured. For a list of insurance definitions, see Fig. 16-2.

In your comparative study of insurers, while some consideration should be given to cost, more should be given to whether the policies are sufficiently broad to supply all coverage and whether the company will serve you adequately in time of loss. Some insurers may charge a lower initial premium; those that charge a higher premium may pay a dividend.

Rule of thumb

The average annual cost is from one to four percent of the value of the insured property. Insurance against damage or loss of property should be for replacement value.

"Co-insurance" means risk shared by the property owner and insurance company. Major protection is given to the owner. The premium is considerably

BENEFICIARY—person designated to receive face amount of policy

CASH VALUE OF POLICY—amount insurance company will pay if policy is canceled (generally a life insurance policy)

COVERAGE—type of loss for which policy will pay

DEDUCTIBLES—specified dollar amount and percentage of loss above which the insurance company will pay

FACE AMOUNT OF POLICY—life insurance term: amount paid by insurance company in case of death of insured

EXCLUSIONS—types of losses for which policy will not pay

INDEMNITY—you collect only the actual amount of loss and not amount named in policy as policy limit

LIMITATIONS—maximum amount of payment provided by policy

PREMIUM—amount paid to keep policy in force

SUBROGATION—insured gives insurer right of recovery against liable third party to extent that insurer indemnifies insured for loss

Fig. 16-2. Insurance Definitions.

lower for co-insurance. You insure at a required level, usually seventy to eighty percent of the actual property value, and you are insured for all claims below that amount. The insurance company pays for losses in full up to the face value of the policy.

For example, if the requirement is eighty percent insurance under the co-insurance clause, you are required to carry $80,000 for insurance of property valued at $100,000; the insurance company is liable for the full amount up to $80,000 and you bear the loss of $20,000.

Comprehensive policies incorporate a variety of covering clauses. Discuss these all-risk contracts with your agent; they may be the most economical and give the most coverage.

Review with the agent the risks to which your business may be exposed, the costs should these mishaps occur, and the cost of insurance coverage. Having decided what to insure, then determine the best methods and their premiums and limitations as well as the coverage of each policy. Use as high a deductible as you can afford. Buy package policies whenever suitable.

The types of insurance with which you'll be most concerned are fire, liability, automobile, workers' compensation, and perhaps crime.

Fire insurance

The standard fire insurance policy pays only for losses due directly to fire, lightning, and losses due to temporary removal of goods from the premises because of fire. The policy with an extended-coverage endorsement at relatively little cost may insure against damage from hail, windstorm, explosion, riot, aircraft, vehicle, smoke, vandalism, and malicious mischief. A co-insurance clause reduces the premium.

A fire insurance policy might also be augmented by business-interruption coverage. The indirect loss could be worse than the direct loss. Indirect loss could be: loss of use of building; continuing expenses such as rent or salaries; cost of temporary quarters; loss of customer property, for example, items left for repair or for cleaning. Rental property which becomes unusable should be landlord-insured.

Liability insurance

Liability insurance protects against claims of others for physical injury to persons on your premises and damage to their property; it may also cover personal injuries such as libel and slander. It also covers liability for products and defects in merchandise. General liability insurance is very important because you are legally responsible for negligence that harms customers, employees, and anyone else with whom you do business. You may be legally liable even when you use reasonable care. You may be liable to trespassers. General comprehensive liability insurance may not cover everything; for example, it does not cover product liability, and such insurance is becoming increasingly important.

Give thought to possible liability for products you sell. Get guidance from your attorney. Stay current on the legal status of your merchandise, including fabrics that are flammable, food, and drugs.

Casualty insurance

Casualty insurance covers loss of property because of destruction or damage, or dishonesty. It covers the following disasters: fire, lightning, windstorm, flood, hail, earthquake, tornado, riot, vandalism, malicious mischief, explosion, smoke, and water damage. Dishonesty covers automobile theft, burglary, robbery, theft, and forgery.

Comprehensive property insurance does not cover automobiles, cash, or jewelry; they are protected by another type of policy. It is an all-risk policy which covers all perils except those specifically excluded. The total premium of an all-risk policy is generally less than the same coverage by several policies. You avoid gaps because of omissions, and you are less likely to duplicate coverage.

A commercial multi-peril policy does not cover floods. A separate policy covers against such risks as overflowing rivers and ground seepage from underground springs. Water damage applies only to such causes as leaking pipes, roofs, and burst water tanks.

Crime insurance

Crime insurance is expensive, and your need for it depends upon your kind of business and its location. Types of crime such as burglary, robbery, and theft by employees can be included in a comprehensive all-risk policy available to small businesses. If you are in a high-crime area and crime insurance available to you is excessively costly, you may get help from the federal crime insurance plan. Your agent can advise you about this.

Automobile insurance

You are required to maintain insurance on all automobiles or other vehicles you operate for your business, and you can be legally liable for accidents by vehicles owned by others—employees, vendors or others—who are involved in accidents while using their vehicles on behalf of your business. Insurance carried on automobiles should cover both collision and public liability. You can carry the business car under the family car insurance policy if your business is a sole proprietorship. Trucks are not eligible under the family policy.

Automobile liability covers owned, rented, and borrowed vehicles. A full-coverage policy pays all losses in full; a deductible policy carries lower premiums but provides that the owner be responsible for the first $50 or $100 or more in damage from the accident, depending upon the policy.

Automobile medical payments insurance pays for claims including your own from car accidents regardless of questions of negligence. Personal property stored in the car and not attached to it, merchandise for example, is not covered by automobile insurance.

Glass insurance

Glass insurance covers plate glass windows and lettering on glass, and the cost of temporarily boarding up windows when necessary. It also covers glass showcases.

Business interruption insurance

Business interruption insurance provides additional coverage for expenses such as:

1. fixed expenses and also lost profits, interest
2. loss if the supplier is closed down by peril
3. amounts you pay to hurry up the reopening of your business
4. serious disruption short of closing
5. loss of supply of power, light, heat, water

Employee insurance

The employer's liability to employees relates to their health and safety while on duty. Workers compensation is employer liability insurance dictated by the law, requiring that the employer provide a safe place to work, safe tools, and warning of existing dangers. State statutes govern the kind of benefits payable to workers.

Surety bonds guarantee that employees and others with whom you transact business are honest and will fulfill contractual obligations, for example, a contractor engaged by you to remodel your store building.

Fidelity bonds are purchased for employees occupying positions that involve handling of company funds.

Life insurance on key employees, payable to the company, is protection against losses from owners' or partners' premature death, disability, or medical expenses. The business has an insurable interest in the lives of its key employees, and this can be charged as a business expense.

A business can buy or help buy group life and health insurance for employees.

Minimizing risks

The insurance program should be reviewed annually. Periodic appraisal of all insured property is important.

Some risks you can minimize or eliminate. Some risks you absorb because they are uncontrollable, but good planning protects against them. You can remove causes of accidents such as fire hazards, water damage, slippery floors, and dangerous sidewalks. To safeguard against robbery and burglary consider the layout of the store, including cash register location, and take precautions such as installing proper locks on doors, metal bars on windows.

For security's sake, establish set routines for opening and closing the store, an established pattern of starting at the same door to lock up and starting at the same switch when turning off the lights; as well as looking into dressing rooms, washrooms, and storage areas.

Insurance companies reduce premiums if yours is an E safe. Bolt your safe to the building; put it where it can be seen from the street; and have a light on it. Never leave the combination on the store premises; if an employee who knows

Agent

Policies

Company	Liability	Amount	Premium Amount	Due date
	fire			
	liability			
	casualty			
	vehicles			
	crime			
	comprehensive			
	business interruption			
	glass			
	surety bonds			
	fidelity			
	employee group health, life			

Fig. 16-3. Insurance Record.

the combination leaves your employ, change the combination. Some safes have an inner compartment with a special slot for cash deposits; only the owner has access to this second compartment.

Insurance recordkeeping

The insurance record should list each policy, number, name and address of agent, type of coverage, amount and due date of premium, expiration date. Keep a list of all insured equipment, including model number, purchase date, and price. Figure 16-3 presents a sample insurance record.

17

Who owns the store?

WEIGH THE ADVANTAGES AND DISADVANTAGES IN DETERMINING WHETHER YOU will operate the business as a sole owner, whether you will take a partner or partners, or whether you will incorporate. Each has advantages and disadvantages.

Sole proprietorship
Advantages

A sole proprietorship is the least expensive of all types of business organization, and the simplest to start and terminate. You need only acquire an occupational license and an employer's identification number from the designated federal and state departments. Management is centralized in the owner. All profits are the owner's. The business is fully transferable should the owner wish to be divested of it. Business earnings are taxed as part of the owner's personal income at a personal income tax rate; however, an additional form itemizing income and expenditures of the business must be filed. Business losses and expenses are tax deductible by the owner.

Disadvantages

A disadvantage of sole proprietorship is the unlimited personal liability of the owner. Another drawback is that the amount of available capital and extent of obtainable credit are limited to the owner's financial resources.

The sole proprietor need not pay or withhold Social Security taxes on spouse-employee wages. Dividing the small business's income between husband

and wife is less than the self-employment tax the sole proprietor must pay on his own self-employment income; however the employee-spouse who is not covered under the Social Security Act will not be earning credits toward Social Security benefits. A lesser-earning self-employed spouse will not compile as many Social Security benefits for himself.

Partnership
Advantages

A partnership is ownership by two or more persons or entities. It is actually a business owned by a number of sole proprietors. All partners have equal voice in management of the business; they share equally in profits and losses. There are general and limited partnerships.

Disadvantages

It is difficult to dispose of a partnership business. A two member partnership dissolves with the death or withdrawal of one of the partners. Interest in the partnership business is transferable but the rights of a partner are not; the assignee cannot participate in the management unless he is taken into the business as a partner.

A partnership business is not taxed but, as in a sole proprietorship, it must file a form itemizing income and expenses of the business. The partners are taxed as part of their personal income. In other words, there are no double taxes, a situation in which both the corporation and stockholders each pay taxes. Liability is unlimited; every partner is liable personally for company debts and for judgments. The creditor can collect from any partner, regardless of which partner contracted the debt, in proportion to the amount each partner contributed to the business. The recourse that the other partners have in such an event is to sue the partner who contracted the debt. To protect the business from such occurrence and other eventualities there should be a written partnership agreement.

Partnership agreement

Few formalities are necessary in setting up a partnership; you do need a business license from the county or city clerk. Nevertheless, it is wise to formulate articles of partnership, drawn up by an attorney. In the process of formulation, agreements are made and understandings reached that forestall future problems. The agreement should include: allocations of profit and loss, identification of property contributed and loaned; management and check-writing authority; rules relating to dissolution, withdrawal, or liquidation; and tax allocation. See Fig. 17-1, necessary terms of articles of partnership.

In the absence of a written partnership agreement, the Iowa Uniform Partnership Act, for example, directs that profits and losses be shared equally. It is imperative that your attorney acquaint you with the laws of your state relating to partnerships.

It is particularly important in a partnership that there be specific assignments of responsibilities and authority—who does the purchasing, who supervises and

Date

Name of business

Name and address of each partner

General or limited partnership

Status of the various partners

Duration of partnership from beginning date

Amount of investment of each partner, whether in money or property

Duties of each partner

Compensation of each partner and additional provisions for consideration

Drawing account of each partner

Matters pertaining to admission of new partners, withdrawal of existing partners, and terms and notice requirements

Ultimate dissolution of partnership

Division of profits and losses—drawing and/or salaries

Employment management

Sale of partnership interests

Arbitration and settlement of disputes

Required and prohibited acts

Absence or disability of partners

Addition, alteration, or modification of partnership agreement

Buy-sell agreement

Decision-making procedure, each in partner's area of operation

Who is responsible for records, audit

Who signs checks

Extent to which each partner can pledge credit

Surviving spouses, children, heirs

Rules for expelling partner

When meetings shall be held

Amount of time each partner agrees to devote to business

Provision for continuation of business by remaining partners in event of death or other dissolution and method for appraisal and payment of interest of deceased or former partner

Fig. 17-1. Necessary Terms of Articles of Partnership.

gives orders to employees and who signs checks. To preserve smooth operation of the business, make definite rules, and define shared responsibilities before the business is opened.

As a business consultant I have found it difficult, when first meeting with two friends who enthusiastically are planning a new business together, to advise that they first draw up a legal partnership agreement. I have found it even more difficult to counsel an established partnership that has never had a written agreement defining duties and privileges of each partner, and dollar value of nonmonetary input of each.

A children's bookstore was started as somewhat of a lark by two women who had their own careers elsewhere. May Burton was a kindergarten teacher, and Sue Evans was an office manager. Their first "bookstore" consisted of shelves in May's dining room. Business hours were weekends and two weekday evenings. Because the store was in her home, May handled customer relations and housekeeping. Sue kept the records, paid the bills, maintained the book inventory, and wrote the advertising. She did much of the work in her own home, where she had her computer, typewriter, office equipment, and records.

The business grew. It became a bookstore in a downtown location, with regular business hours of the area and a part-time salesperson.

However, the partners discovered as they worked together that they had separate abilities, which they respected, but that they also had separate ideas, which was less tolerable. I was engaged as a consultant.

The problem I was asked to consider was, on first glance, a simple one, relating to the buying of the books. Sue, with her eye on figures, felt that investment in new books should observe strictly the budget amount as agreed upon in each category: picture books, books for reading aloud, fiction for various age groups, and nonfiction. If sales were slow in a particular category, replenishment should heed the inventory signals. May felt that each semiannual book-buying season called for new books in every category, and she wanted the privilege of buying sessions even between markets, should a supplier come into the store to display his new titles. May believed she should have the privilege of using her own judgment, even if it did not always conform to inventory red lights.

As the partners explained the problem I sensed a "hidden agenda." May seemed to resent long hours "on the floor," housekeeping, and maintenance duties, and lack of buying authority when she was working with a supplier. Sue seemed to feel that May did not understand the amount of time necessary for the office end of the business; when she was taking stock inventory she should not be interrupted to wait on a customer.

I also learned that there had been no written statement relating to termination of the business, nor any indication of the dollar value of nonmonetary items owned by a partner and being used by the business.

There was no expressed acrimony, but the buildup threatened the life of a business in which the partners had invested time and money—successfully. My role was that of arbitrator in the dialogue between the partners. It was after the total meeting of their minds that their attorney drew up a written partnership agreement. The bookstore continues to flourish.

Limited partnership

A limited partner does not participate in management of the store. Should he enter into the management, he loses his limited liability. If he has day-to-day responsibility, he cannot call himself a limited partner.

Limited partners have the limited liability that stockholders in corporations have, but the advantage is that they pay taxes as do all other partners and the partnership itself is not taxed. Their income from the business is reported on their personal income tax return. Their interest in the profits of the business is assignable to anyone they elect. They may withdraw from the business with six-month's notice. Thus a limited partner can provide revenue without unlimited liability.

A limited partnership must file a certificate of limited partnership with the state. This certificate should include the name of the limited partnership, general character of its business, address of principal place of business, name and address of agent for service of process, name and address of each partner (specifying general partners and limited partners), description and value of contributions by each partner, rules regarding dissolution, and assignment of interests.

Corporation

A corporation is a body of persons granted a charter by the state in which it does business, recognizing it as a separate entity with its own rights, privileges, and liabilities distinct from those of its members; it is a legal person and business entity. As a legal entity it owns the assets and is liable for the debts. It must file articles of incorporation with the secretary of the state. Management is by its board of directors and officers elected by the shareholders. There must be an annual meeting of the officers and stockholders; minutes must be kept of this and all other meetings as proof that the directors carry out corporate business according to purposes as sanctioned by the state.

Shareholders' liability is limited to their capital contribution, but personal guaranty of the corporation debt may be required by creditors. Officers and directors may receive salaries as employees, and fees as officers and directors. Stock is transferable freely, subject to securities regulation.

Advantages

The advantages of incorporation are limited liability of stockholders, perpetual life of the company, ease of transferring ownership by stockholders, greater ability to raise capital. A larger number of shareholders usually brings not only more capital to the firm, but also influence, which enhances the firm's image.

Disadvantages

The disadvantages of a corporation are:

1. Its activities are limited to those specifically granted in the charter, unless a catch-all clause granting unlimited scope has been included in the charter.

2. Its geographical area of operation is limited to the state granting its charter until permission is granted from other states in which it wishes to operate. This means additional license fees must be paid and additional regulations observed.

3. If management is employed in lieu of owner-management, the personal incentive associated with ownership is lessened.

4. A corporation is subject to more taxes than a proprietorship or partnership, unless it elects to be taxed as though it were a partnership under Subchapter S of the Internal Revenue Code. Both corporation and its stockholders pay taxes.

5. Because of federal and state regulations, more reports and records are necessary for taxation and other purposes, and corporations are facing increasing federal and state regulations.

6. In small corporations the advantage of limited liability is often circumvented by creditors who require that major stockholders guarantee or endorse original notes.

Subchapter S corporations

Subchapter S corporations are corporations that elect not to be taxed as corporations. Instead, the shareholders, as though it were a partnership, include in their individual gross incomes their proportionate shares of corporate profits and losses. To qualify as a Subchapter S corporation, a business must be a domestic corporation, have only one class of stock, not be a member of an affiliated group, have not more than a specified number of stockholders (which at present is thirty-five, husband and wife and their estates counting as one), have only individuals or estates as shareholders, and be owned by United States citizens.

Forming a corporation

Regulations relative to forming a corporation are dictated by the state. It is advisable to have the services of a lawyer experienced in that area of business law.

The first step is the preparation of a certificate of incorporation. Most states require that it be prepared by three or more legally qualified persons, and that it designate names and addresses of persons who will serve as interim directors until the first meeting of the corporation. If it is acceptable by the designated state official, a charter is issued; the stockholders must meet at a designated place and time to complete the incorporation process. It's advisable to have present the attorney or someone else familiar with corporate organizational procedure. At that time the bylaws are adopted (if they have not already been submitted with the articles of incorporation) and the board of directors is elected. This board elects the officers, who will have charge of the corporation. The officers must include at least a president, secretary, and treasurer. In small corporations the members of the board frequently are elected as officers of the corporation.

In forming a corporation, members of the board of directors should be selected carefully. They, and not the stockholders, govern the corporation's action. Avoid naming relatives unless they can contribute to decision-making. On a five member board, the usual size, it is efficient to have one lawyer and one certified public accountant. It is imperative to hold real, rather than faked, board meetings, properly and regularly scheduled. The lawyer on the board should keep other members aware of federal and state legislation governing corporations.

To sell capital stock, refer to your charter to know the amount of stock you are permitted to sell. An investment banker will handle the sale of stock. His fee can be amortized over a number of years, and it is charged to the corporation's expenses. Hold back a number of shares for possible future financing of expansion.

See Fig. 17-2 for articles of incorporation.

Contents

Corporate name

Purpose for which corporation was formed

Length of time for which corporation is formed

Names and addresses of incorporators

Location of principal office in state of incorporation

Amount and type of capital stock to be authorized

Capital required at time of incorporation

Names and addresses of interim directors until first meeting of shareholders, when their successors will be selected

By-Laws

May repeat above provisions

Location of principal office and other offices of corporation

Date and place of stockholders' meetings and provision for calling and conducting meetings

Necessary quorum for stockholders' meetings

Voting privileges of stockholders

Number of directors, method of electing them, method of creating or filling vacancies on board of directors

Time and place of directors' meetings and requirements for quorum of directors

Method of electing officers, their duties, terms of office, salaries

Stock certificates, their transfer, their control in company books

Right to declare dividends

Fig. 17-2. Articles of Incorporation, By-Laws.

Choosing the legal structure

We go back now to the opening question of this chapter: Who owns the store? So far it is your store, your dream business. You are aware now that there are both advantages and disadvantages of several kinds of ownership. It is an old quip that if you want to grow, don't make your business a sole proprietorship. However, as you give consideration to a partnership or a corporation, ask yourself if at this stage it might be wise to postpone the alternatives of shared ownership.

Perhaps you are considering taking on a partner because of your need for capital. In that event, why not take on not a full partner, but a limited partner who would put money in the business, and have no voice in the management but have full profit-sharing advantages?

To again quote the wise counselor, a friendship and a business affiliation cannot survive together. To follow such advice would be to avoid close friends or relatives as partners—and also as major stockholders. There can be but one captain of the ship.

In a corporation, consider the matter of nonvoting stock. Sell shares if you need the money, but keep controlling interest in the number of shares you own, and at the very outset have yourself elected as president or manager. Avoid giving stock to employees; give them plaques, promotions, fancy titles, and gifts. The stock may end up in the hands of people who have no real interest in the business and want dividends and not earning retention, important for corporation expansion. If you do give stock to employees, have a buy-sell agreement that states that if they stop working for the company, they must sell the stock back to the company at an agreed-upon price.

Federal income tax

For a sole proprietorship or partnership, your income tax is that of an individual, but you file an additional form, Schedule C of 1040, Profit or Loss from Business or Profession. In a partnership, you file a return showing income and expenses of the business, and each partner reports only his share of profit on his own return.

As sole proprietor or partner, you must pay federal income tax and self-employment tax as income is received. You do this by filing a Declaration of Estimated Tax, Form 1040 ES on or before April 15 of each year as the estimate of income and self-employment taxes you expect to owe based on expected income and exemptions. You pay this estimate each quarter: April 15, June 15, September 15, and January 15. At the time of each payment, adjustments to the estimate may be made.

Income tax returns for corporations are due on the fifteenth day of the third month following the end of each taxable year. A corporation's taxable year need not coincide with the calendar year.

As an owner of a new business you may be required to file a declaration on a date other than April 15.

Subchapter S corporations have the advantages of both corporations and partnerships. They avoid the double-tax feature of corporations; they permit shareholders to offset corporation losses against their own income. However, if a Subchapter S corporation has substantial profits, personal taxes will be higher than the maximum corporate tax.

In whatever structure of business, credits against federal income tax are not actually tax deductions. They account for much more than that; they are allowed for qualified investment in certain equipment and specially defined energy and recycling devices.

18

Financial planning

YOU HAVE FINALIZED MUCH OF YOUR PLANNING—WHAT YOU WILL SELL, TO whom, from what location; and you have determined your marketing strategy—how you will reach your customers. Knowing your sales-center needs, you know the cost of buying, renting, or erecting such a building, the cost of furniture and equipment, remodeling, and redecorating. By coordinating and applying the results of your study, you are ready to express your business goals in terms of dollars and cents. You must now determine how much start-up capital you'll need and where it will come from.

Determining your funding needs

Capital is money. It is also money equivalents: the building, if you already own or are buying it; equipment that you already own—files, typewriters, computers, desks, sewing machines, refrigerators, and trucks. Capital investment also includes securities the business may own. Money is the most important item of your capital investment because it can be converted into capital goods that the business needs, for example, furniture, fixtures, counters, and merchandise.

Make a list of your capital investment—the items needed for starting your business and their costs. Keep in separate lists the fixed assets and current assets. Remember, assets are all of the things, small as well as large, that a business needs to be able to operate. Assets are subdivided into current assets and fixed assets. Current assets are resources that can readily be converted into cash, as well as cash itself; they include also inventory and short lived items, which for the most part are consumed as part of the selling process of the inventory. Fixed assets are those items that are important to the business' operation but are not for sale to the store's customers; their lifetime is more than one year—furniture, fixtures, equipment, trucks, and machinery. Alteration and decoration of the premises being prepared for occupancy may be included in fixed assets if they are to be paid for by you, the tenant.

To estimate how much money you will need for starting your store, add together the cost of the assets you will need and estimated operating expenses for the first three months. See Figs. 18-1 through 18-5.

Calculating your own resources

Estimate how much money you have and how much you can afford or are willing to risk. You find the answer by listing all of your living expenses and comparing the total with your estimated drawing amount from the business. Do not expect to make a profit for the first three months; extend your computation for an additional nine months. Will this amount be adequate to cover your living expenses? Do you have other plans for income? Your business-affordable drawing amount must match your personal income requirements or you will have to look to other sources.

When you consider borrowing money, remember that the less borrowing you do, the less interest you will have to pay, and the less collateral you will need.

Harry Firestone, the international merchant, is quoted as having said, "I lacked capital. Because of this I was forced to keep down overhead, and to watch every expenditure. I found it necessary to study details, to eliminate waste."

Ways to reduce expenses

Expenses might be reduced. Your own labor may be a substitute for money spent for salaries, for redecorating and carpentry. Perhaps the investment in inventory can be reduced. There is a tendency for a novice entrepreneur to overbuy.

For fixture and furniture buying, consider various avenues for economy:

1. Postpone the purchase of some of the assets on your list.
2. Get price estimates from several sources, and get prices for both new and used items.
3. Buy on a two year contract, thus making one-half or more of the balance due a fixed liability rather than a current liability, which must be paid in a year.
4. When buying on contract, you may be able to make a modest down payment, and monthly payments over a period of several years. Bear in mind, however, that such payments for long-term assets are not considered operating expense and must be made out of net profits of an established business, out of investment capital for a new business. Care must be taken that monthly payments do not exceed the business's profit.

Salesroom   Cost

counters   _____

showcases   _____

display tables   _____

shelving   _____

cash register   _____

carpeting   _____

lighting fixtures   _____

installation of shelving, fixtures   _____

other items   _____

Workroom

shelving   _____

tables   _____

chairs   _____

price marking equipment   _____

sign printer   _____

fixture installation costs   _____

other items   _____

Office

desks   _____

chairs   _____

files   _____

typewriters   _____

Fig. 18-1. Fixed Assets.

computer   _____

calculator   _____

bookkeeping machine   _____

copier   _____

postage meter   _____

mailing scale   _____

other items   _____

Cleaning Equipment

vacuum cleaner   _____

other items   _____

Remodeling and Redecorating

renovation   _____

remodeling   _____

redecorating   _____

Total fixed assets   _____

Fig. 18-1. Continued.

5. Convert assets you already own from personal to business use, thus making them part of your business owner's equity; you may already own such usable items as a desk, typewriter, and pickup truck.

6. Instead of buying some of your equipment, consider leasing it with option to buy. Rent is tax deductible, which in itself is a bonus.

7. You may be able to get some of your merchandise on consignment, payable as you sell the items, with the privilege of returning unsold portions. Very large companies sometimes use this method; why not you?

ITEM	Percent of operating expense
rent	_____
utilities, installation and use	_____
salaries and payroll, including owner	_____
advertising, somewhat higher than afterward	_____
supplies	_____
repairs and maintenance	_____
professional fees	_____
licenses and other fees	_____
insurance	_____
interest on loans	_____
payment on equipment bought on contract	_____
payment for inventory for which credit was given by vendors	_____
inventory replenishment	_____
contingencies (unanticipated expenditures, 15% - 25%)	_____

Fig. 18-2. Start-Up Operating Expenses for First Three Months.

8. You can try to get vendors of merchandise and equipment to give you extended credit for thirty to ninety days, hopefully interest free, with the expectation that you'll have money coming in from sales as soon as your business doors open.

By buying merchandise on regular credit terms but in limited quantity and selling it for cash, you can count on its rapid sale before paying the vendors and before interest is due.

Summary

What I need:

A.   Assets current and fixed _____

B.   Operating expenses for three months _____

    C.   Working capital _____

What I have:

D.   Cash investment available _____

E.   Fixed assets already owned _____

    F.   Total available capital _____

If C is less than F—I need no outside funding resource.

If C is more than F—I need outside funding resource.

Fig. 18-3. Start-Up Working Capital.

By being resourceful, by watching expenses, you can keep operation costs down. By being alert to cash flow, you will know your cash status when bills come due. Paying bills on time is particularly vital to a new business; it's your way of establishing your credit. Before asking for credit from vendors or bankers, it is expedient to have established your credit rating: a savings account and a checking account in your name, credit cards, and an established record of having paid your bills promptly.

Chattel mortgage: lien on such items of personal property as trucks, cash registers

Real estate mortgage: on real property

Savings account: bank keeps passbook for the account

Life insurance policies: rather than borrowing directly from the insurance company, it may be more convenient and less costly to assign the policy to the bank and borrow money up to the cash value of the policy.

Stocks, bonds: must be marketable to be used as collateral; if stock drops below bank's required value, it may request additional security.

Trust receipts: where collateral is merchandise, such as cars and appliances, which have to be displayed to be sold, owner promises to pay the bank as the goods are sold.

Warehouse receipts: bank takes readily marketable merchandise as collateral.

Accounts receivable: with a notification plan, charge account customers pay their bills to the bank; with a non-notification plan, charge account customers pay their bill to the store and the store pays the bank.

Insurance policies

Fig. 18-4. Collateral as Guarantee of Loan Payment.

Personal Capital Worth

I Own*		I Owe	
cash	$_____	charge accounts	$_____
securities	$_____		$_____
	$_____		$_____
real estate	$_____	other payables	$_____
	$_____		$_____
automobiles	$_____	car payment	$_____
	$_____	mortgage payment	$_____
home furnishings	$_____	other liabilities	$_____
other assets	$_____		$_____
	$_____		$_____
Total assets	$_____	Total liabilities	$_____

Personal Monthly Budget

rent	$_____
mortgage	_____
loan	_____
car payments	_____
car maintenance	_____
car insurance	_____
house insurance	_____
personal property insurance	_____
house maintenance	_____
utilities	_____
life and health insurance	_____
household expenses	_____
clothing	_____
children's education	_____
other expenses	_____

Total monthly expenses $_____   Monthly income $_____

---

*List all assets at actual market worth today.
**Subtract liabilities from assets or vice versa; the resulting figure is your net worth.

Fig. 18-5. Personal Financial Budget.

One way to establish your credit before going into business is to get a small loan from a bank and pay it back before it comes due; the interest will cost you next to nothing if you deposit the loan in an interest-paying bank account. Wait a few months and then apply for a loan of a larger amount than the previous one; again pay it back before it comes due.

After all of your planning for reducing your anticipated expenses, should you still find your own resources to be inadequate, there are a variety of sources for getting funds without having to borrow.

Equity funding

Equity funding is the name for getting money for your business by selling a part of the ownership to investors who may or may not participate in the management. You do this by taking a partner or by selling stock. By forming a partnership or a corporation, you sell part of the interest in the business to people who are willing to risk their money; they will not be paid back the amount of their investment but they hope to get it back by sharing in the profits. The alternatives to operating as a sole owner are discussed in Chapter 17: Who Owns the Store.

Another source of funding comes from venture capital firms, which invest money in businesses that hold good promise for growth. It is rarely available to very small businesses. These investors would rather see funds reinvested in the business than issued as interest payments.

The disadvantage of equity financing, in addition to having to share the profits, is that you are relinquishing ownership. The advantage of equity financing is that you add to your working capital without increasing your liability. You do not have to pay the money back. In taking a partner you get her capital; you also get her credit rating and her talents.

You can go to private lenders

Borrowed money is a liability to be paid back. You may consider borrowing money from private persons: friends and relatives. If so, be businesslike. Have a lawyer draw up a loan agreement specifying amount, due date for repayment, interest, and any collateral.

A demand note must be paid in full on demand; a wise borrower pays it back as soon as possible. Money loaned at below interest rates is considered a gift, and the lender may have to pay a gift tax. A no-interest demand loan is not considered a gift. Payment of loans are tax deductible by the borrower.

Lending institutions as a funding source

If you plan to go into business with borrowed money, you are not only risking the money of someone else, to whom you are responsible, you are risking your own credit rating—your good name—and you must ask yourself what the odds are that you can repay the loan.

Lending institutions such as banks are interested not only in the loan repayment, but also in borrowers with good profit-making businesses. Banks want to know what you can do for them, not vice versa. They make profit only on good loans, and they want to be certain of repayment. They set restrictions to protect against unnecessary risk and poor business management, especially in making long-term loans. These lending institutions are businesses and have to operate according to certain principles. Both borrower and lender, therefore, must think in terms of earnings, management, and long-range prospects. Earning less than the cost of borrowed money is harmful. For example, if earnings are six percent on total investments and twelve percent is paid out in interest charges, the business is a poor risk for the lender and promises a disastrous future for the borrower.

The lender to a new business usually expects the borrower to invest at least twenty to twenty-five percent of his own money in a business in which the lender is being asked to risk money. The lender will expect the borrower to share the gamble.

Sometimes a lender may require only a signature, or only a financial statement, or endorsers or guarantors, but for the most part, he will require collateral to reduce the risk he is taking. A guarantor guarantees payment of the note if the lender fails to pay. The lender can collect from either the maker of the loan or the guarantor.

The bank establishes the terms—the interest rate, period of the loan, how it is to be repaid—monthly or a lump sum at the end of the period.

The cost of the borrowing debt is the annual percentage rate of interest. Loans are usually at the prevailing rate. For example, you borrow $100 for one year at eight percent; the interest is $8. If it is a discounted loan, you pay the interest in advance. You get $100 less $8 = $92. If it's a discounted installment loan, you will be expected to repay it in twelve monthly installments, thus almost doubling the amount of interest you will pay.

The borrower should see the loan contract in advance of the closing and have legal advice; he should know the lending terms before signing. Once he signs the contract he is bound by it. However, a loan agreement may be amended from time to time.

The kinds of loans available

There are various kinds of loans, depending upon what the loan is for and what the repayment terms consist of. Short-term loans are for financing accounts receivable and for inventory; the bank expects to be paid when the inventory has been converted into cash, when the accounts are paid. Short-term loans may be unsecured, requiring no collateral. Secured loans are those in which the borrower pledges some of the business assets, and are usually for a year or more. Long-terms are usually for equipment and real estate, and are paid back in periodic installments from earnings.

By getting a line of credit from a bank, you reserve the loan to be used when the need arises. You do not pay interest on it during the time that you do not use it. You borrow as the need presents itself; you repay the part borrowed and borrow again. You can get variable interest rates on the amount borrowed.

A revolving loan establishes the maximum amount the business can borrow; you are allowed to borrow repeatedly and then repay as long as the amount due is less than the maximum credit.

In the loan agreement, there are covenants negative and positive. Negative covenants are restrictive—the things that the borrower may not do without approval of the lender. Positive covenants are things that the borrower must do—maintain maximum working capital, have adequate insurance, repay the loan according to the terms, and supply the lender with financial statements.

Applying for a loan

If you are confident in your business and yourself as the operator of the business, you are ready to proceed with a visit to the bank, dressed in your Sunday best, and armed with a well-formulated written presentation.

The loan officer at the bank will ask you a lot of questions; how the money will be spent, if the company is a good risk, and how the money will be repaid.

The financial proposal which you devise preparatory to applying for a loan is much like a business plan. It is actually the result of the research you did when you were formulating your prebusiness plan. However, in a loan application, you itemize a different set of assets than those in your general business plan. You supply only those assets relating to the business, nor does your income report list the expenses.

This financial proposal helps to establish your credibility. It shows others what you want to do, how you plan to do it, how the requested loan if granted will be used, and how it will be repaid.

The banker may require you to provide such information by answering questions on a printed form, or he may find a cover letter acceptable. Such a letter should provide the lender with the financial data that will give him confidence that the money will be paid back. The letter or documentation for a loan application should contain:

1. Description of the business: location, merchandise, customers, amount of loan requested and its purpose, when you will repay the loan, and collateral.

2. Financial information: balance sheet, profit and loss statement, projected financial statement, insurance, business outlook for this business and business in general.

3. Personal information: borrower's creditworthiness, most recent income tax return, source of income, work history, management capabilities, and credit references.

There are a number of questions you should ask the loan officer, bearing in mind that you are a potential client. The bank's income is derived from clients like you. Your business commodity is apparel or flowers or food or bicycles, as the case may be; the banker's commodity happens to be money. You want to buy some of it, for which you plan to give him a profit in the form of additional dollars—interest. When he agrees to the loan, your thanks are a courtesy. Do you thank your grocer? The banker has not given you anything; it was your statistics that got you the loan.

When your future is favorable and your credit is good, you may wish to shop around among other banks for the one offering you the best terms.

The Small Business Administration as a lender

To apply for a Small Business Administration loan, first talk with an SBA officer or your banker and make sure you are eligible. A small business is defined as one independently owned and dominant in a field. There are also size determinants— income and number of employees. SBA will not make loans if funds are otherwise available on reasonable terms. It will not make a loan to a nonprofit enterprise; to the publisher of a newspaper, magazine, or books; or to a radio, television, or investment business.

The procedure for applying for an SBA loan is to take all of your loan application material to a banker and apply for a direct loan. If you are turned down, inquire if the bank is interested in making an SBA-guaranteed loan. If you get an affirmative reply, ask the banker to contact SBA to discuss your application. In most cases SBA will deal directly with the bank. The SBA loan officer evaluates an application on the following criteria:

1. character and debt-paying record of borrower;
2. analysis of financial statements—summary sheet, cash flow projection, past earnings of the business or its earnings potential;
3. value of collateral in terms of market value and liquidity;
4. how much money is being asked for, how it will be used, how repaid;
5. ability to repay.

Should the loan be granted, the bank will guarantee your loan repayment up to a stipulated percentage. The bank sets the interest rate and terms, complying with government rulings.

SBA direct loans, not via a bank, are available to disadvantaged persons such as minorities, the handicapped, veterans, and victims of major catastrophes such as floods. The loans are for a longer period and at a lower interest rate than SBA-guaranteed loans.

Additional funding sources

Commercial finance companies   make loans on the strength of collateral that the borrower owns rather than on the business's operating record. The risks are higher than for bank loans, so the interest rate is usually higher.

Life insurance companies   will loan against life insurance policies up to ninety-five percent of the value of the policy, but until it is repaid the loan is a direct deduction from what the policy is worth. The interest rate is less than for a loan from a bank because less risk is involved. You do not have to pay back the loan to the insurance company.

Credit unions charge lower interest than do banks; they will give a mortgage on a home, but this is not a recommended way to obtain money to open a new business.

Savings and loan companies offer real estate mortgages, customarily for a thirty-year period.

Economic development corporations sponsored by state and local organizations attempt to attract new businesses to their areas. The capital is provided by private sources that make outright loans for longer terms than banks, or buy stock in the new venture. Information is available from state development offices, the area chamber of commerce, or banks.

19

Charting your success

A BUSINESS PLAN IS IMPERATIVE *BEFORE* OPENING THE STORE. IT FORCES YOU, before you take a single step, to look at the business in its entirety, and to consider all start-up aspects. Trouble spots are discovered while they are still "paper mistakes" because the business starts out as a paper plan.

The business plan helps establish reasonable objectives and how to achieve them. It is the chart for reaching financial success. It's financial forecast it provides gives you budgeting guidelines, enabling you to determine amount and kind of appropriate financing. It reveals the highest possible profit you can hope for, and the lowest possible level of income to prepare for. You are provided with insurance against business failure.

The business plan points out weaknesses and how to overcome them. It also points out strengths and how to profit from them—strategies that will facilitate achievement.

By presenting your written business plan to bankers and other financial sources, you are providing them with useful and persuasive information about you and your business. And whenever you require funding, this written document will serve you in this same capacity.

Useful not only for starting a business, written and rewritten as your business progresses, it is a blueprint custom made by you. Because it deals with the future as well as the present, it is flexible and alterable. It describes goals, and at the same time contains safety valves. It continues to be your guide in all operational gestures, a working tool for management, a guide in decision-making. It helps prevent impetuous decisions and plunging into action before having thought through the whole operation.

Drawing up your own business plan

This entire book is, in essence, directed to the process of planning a retail store. During your reading I hope you have noted your own ideas, preparing yourself to design your own business plan.

Filling in the blanks in the business plan that appears in Fig. 19-1—the very act of writing them down—will pinpoint essential elements of your decisions, and will serve as a clarification of your conclusions.

Once they are written down, there is no more need for re-evaluation. You know your course of action relating to the kind of business it will be, procedures that express your goals and your policies.

It is a long-term plan. Short-term planning can be in areas that need flexibility in response to changing conditions.

This business plan will also give you control over unforeseen situations, certain to arise because you've adopted a procedural policy.

Financial data will be useful when you apply for a loan or for credit. You will be ready with a written statement to present to someone that you would like to invest in your business, either as a stockholder or as a partner.

In filling out the business plan form, you will find that each item is directed to the book chapter dealing with the topic.

When you have finished you will already be in control of your own business. The decisions, resulting from your own study and evaluation, are YOURS.

Updating your business plan

The business plan, starting all too often as a blueprint for opening your business, actually also should be the vehicle for guiding its continuing successful operation. It should, therefore, from the very beginning be prepared as a three-to-five-year plan. Periodic analysis of your business performance will guide you in revising the plan to comply with changing circumstances and perhaps even goals.

In one period of operation, you may find yourself considering expanding your business—acquiring larger quarters or an additional store. Your assessment may truly invite consideration of expansion, but also point out weak areas which first should be corrected. Success may have cast a rosy hue which blinded you to your shortcomings.

Someone said, "Plan for failure while you strive for success." Analysis is your examination, not only for assessing weak areas, but also for determining the means of surmounting them.

Mistakes are correctable—you invested in too much merchandise or your expenses got out of hand. Understanding the situation, you can give yourself a fresh start by instituting corrections.

But failures are not always mistakes. They sometimes are the result of uncontrollable circumstances—economic recession, new competition in an area that had no market room for another store of its kind. Rather than merely holding your own even in such circumstances, in itself a threat of stagnation, you received a signal that it is time to breathe a new life into your business.

Resource: Chapter 1

entrepreneur _____

the business

    its name _____

    its merchandise _____

the entrepreneur

    motive for going into business

        financial _____

        security _____

        to be the boss _____

        to adapt career to family responsibilities _____

    skills and experience determining strengths and weaknesses

        education

            related to business _____

            _____

            unrelated to business _____

            _____

        skills

            related to business _____

            _____

            unrelated to business _____

            _____

the customers

    targeting the market _____

    _____

    _____

    competition _____

    _____

Fig. 19-1. The Business Plan.

Resource: Chapter 2

Buying an Established Business

name of business _____

address_____

name of owner_____

address_____

kind of business_____

purchase price $ _____

      includes building $ _____

      inventory (liquidation value) $ _____

      equipment (liquidation value) $ _____

      good will value $ _____

terms of purchase_____

terms of lease or sublease _____

inventory turnover (number of times) _____

return on investment

$$\frac{investment}{net\ profit} = \%$$
before taxes

profit

$$\frac{profit}{sales} = \%$$

capital requirement

      cash or payment on contract $ _____

      cost of negotiating contracts $ _____

      additional inventory $ _____

      start-up expense $ _____

      operating expenses 3 months $ _____

      remodeling and redecorating $ _____

Fig. 19-1. Continued.

           capital requirement $ _____

           less anticipated income 3 months $ _____

              total capital requirement $ _____

Buying a Franchise Business

name

location

purchase price

terms of purchase

terms of lease, sublease, or real estate purchase

capital requirement

    start-up expenses

    purchase of franchise

    inventory

    equipment

    remodeling, redecorating

    operating expenses for 3 months

        start-up expense

        less anticipated income for 3 months

           Capital requirement

anticipated profit

    profit ÷ sales = _____%

    investment ÷ net profit before taxes = return on investment of _____%

Resources: Chapters 3 and 4

Location

area

    commercial _____

    commercial strip _____

Fig. 19-1. Continued.

shopping mall _____

residential _____

other _____

building

total size_____

selling space _____

office space _____

work space _____

warehouse space _____

restrooms and employee lounge _____

entrances

front _____

back _____

steps up to entrance _____

parking

meter _____

lot _____

restricted _____

unrestricted _____

traffic flow

good _____ fair _____ minor _____

renovation and redecoration

cost $ _____

responsibility of building owner _____ or tenant _____

purchase of business

price $ _____

down payment $ _____

mortgage terms _____

Fig. 19-1. Continued.

leased by business owner

    rental fee $ _____

    length of lease _____

    obligations of lessor

        repairs _____

        decoration _____

        insurance _____

        other _____

Resources: Chapters 5 and 6

Management and Operation

                              payroll expenses

    owner's salary _____ draw _____   _____

    manager's salary _____ bonus _____   _____

    employees full-time

        salespersons salary _____ commission _____   _____

        office, clerical   _____

        maintenance   _____

        other   _____

    employees part-time

        sales   _____

        office, clerical   _____

        maintenance   _____

        other   _____

        Payroll expenses total   _____

professional assistance

    type   financial terms

    CPA or bookkeeper   _____

Fig. 19-1. Continued.

    attorney   _____

    marketing research   _____

    advertising agency   _____

Resource: Chapter 7

Sales Policy

price

    markup over cost _____ %

    first clearance markdown _____ %

    second _____ %

    third _____ %

credit to customers

    store charge account _____

    Visa _____ MasterCharge _____ American Express _____ other _____

    carrying charge for overdue accounts _____ %

merchandise returns by customers

    refunds

        cash _____ credit _____ exchanges _____

        time limit _____

        sales slips required _____

store hours _____

Resource: Chapter 9

Advertising Media	Start-up budget	Annual budget
television		
_____	_____	_____
_____	_____	_____

Fig. 19-1. Continued.

radio

_____   _____   _____

_____   _____   _____

newspapers, periodicals

_____   _____   _____

_____   _____   _____

mailers

_____   _____   _____

_____   _____   _____

promotions

_____   _____   _____

_____   _____   _____

other

_____   _____   _____

_____   _____   _____

Resource: Chapter 10

The Merchandise

special features

nature of the demand for your product

Suppliers

Name	Credit terms	Advertising allowance	Other benefits

amount

opening inventory

first three months

average annual inventory

Fig. 19-1. Continued.

Resource: Chapter 17

Ownership of Business

sole proprietor

name _____

address _____

partnership

name	general	limited	investment terms
_____	____	____	____
_____	____	____	____
_____	____	____	____

corporation
officers

	position	investment
_____	_____	_____
_____	_____	_____
_____	_____	_____

Subchapter S
officers

_____	_____	_____
_____	_____	_____
_____	_____	_____

Partnership

a data sheet for each partner

skills and experience

    education

    business experience

    skills

financial status

    capital worth

Fig. 19-1. Continued.

capital available for investment in business

capital available as collateral guarantee

cash value   item

personal budget requirements

credit rating

excellent _____ good _____ fair _____ none _____

credit references

character references

Resource: Chapter 18

Funding

start-up capital requirements

equipment _____

inventory _____

start-up expenses _____

operating expenses for three months _____

Total start-up capital requirement _____

personal cash and cash equivalents for business investment

cash and investments _____

real estate _____

equipment _____

inventory _____

Total _____

outside funding

amount needed _____

Fig. 19-1. Continued.

Resources

name   amount   terms

_____   _____   _____

_____   _____   _____

Collateral

name   cash value

_____   _____

_____   _____

_____   _____

credit references

_____

_____

character references

_____

_____

personal budget requirements _____

capital available for investment in business _____

credit rating:

excellent _____ good _____ fair _____ none _____

Fig. 19-1. Continued.

In other words the business plan, updated, is an agenda for action. It is structured for continuous business success.

The warning signs and what to do about them

Your financial records tell you what each next step may be: to sit tight, to expand, or to push alarm buttons in specific areas of your operation.

Should your sales and profits decline, look for the causes and find ways to correct them. Controllable threatening situations call for speedy reaction on your part. A changed environment may call for an entirely new image.

Jacobsons of West Des Moines had that experience. It started out as a workingman's clothing store in a rural, largely blue-collar town. The payroll came from railroad shops and two cement plants, and the farm families were customers as well. The railroad shops moved away, and the cement plants languished when building construction fell off. Fortunately for Jacobsons and an enterprising real estate company, the small town evolved into suburbia, the bedroom town of the nearby city. Many new small homes were made available for purchase. Jacobsons moved into its new building from its long time location near the railroad tracks—a move of just one city block, but an enormous pedestrian character change. It had become a family store, carrying an established reputation of integrity and quality merchandise at reasonable prices. The ownership remained the same—a family with city loyalty and pride that expressed itself in community involvement. Other merchants followed the pattern that had been set. The taverns became restaurants, and the secondhand clothing and furniture stores became antique shops. It was the start of a "downtown" suburban business district, retaining the flavor of Valley Junction, its founding name.

Not necessarily as big an overhaul as this, but a small device may act as a shot-in-the-arm. For example, you might rejuvenate sales with a monthly newsletter. A children's bookstore sends out such a letter, containing reviews not only of books but also of children's magazines and games. Substance rather than style is emphasized; the writing, clear and concise, is a call to action: buy books for your children.

Prospects can be turned into customers, and customers signify repeat business. Try bold and brassy statements about your store and products on billboards, bus stop benches and even on the back of the buses.

No hits, no runs, no errors. If this describes the status quo of your business, you may not be just holding your own; it may be that your business is floundering. No growth may be the first step toward decay. An early sign of trouble is financial insecurity.

Study your overhead expenses, and reassess the amount of money you are drawing out of the business to pay personal expenses. Study your inventory expenditures and turnover.

You may have borrowed too much from the bank, burdening yourself with too much interest expense. If you are meeting the problem of lack of working capital, you might have made an exaggerated projection of anticipated sales income. Had you borrowed only what you had actually needed, and no more at that time, via a demand note from the bank, you would be paying less interest on your original bank loan.

Examine your payroll and the possible need for reducing its size and giving more work to those employees you plan to retain, compensating for the added workload with salary increases.

Expanding your business

Things have gone well, and you are contemplating expanding your business—enlarged quarters or a second store. It might be wise, first, to consider gaining more space in your present location and adding more departments or items by ridding the present shelves of non-selling or non-profitmaking items, and replacing them with "earning items." Drop merchandise carried by discount houses, slow-selling sizes or colors or styles, low-profit departments. Gone is the day of trying to be all things to all people. You are in business to make money.

Opening a second store may entail more than duplicating Store Number One. It will be in another location. Its customers may have different requirements. And away from the "flagship" store, its operation will undoubtedly differ.

Doubling sales with this second outlet will not necessarily mean doubling profits; expenses will go up and usually not in proportion to additional anticipated profit.

If you need more capital

You may need more capital to finance your expansion. You might get fresh money by going back to sources that turned you down before—a bank, venture capital, or a person you contemplated taking in as a partner or as a manager.

Apply for a loan that will fill your needs; base it on your unexaggerated anticipated annual revenue for the next three to five years of your expanded program. Your new presentation must give credibility, figures that support your pledge of repayment: collateral value, credit references, a convincing market study.

The Bank Loan   Figure on keeping the money as long as possible by negotiating a long-term loan with less frequent repayment—two years instead of one, quarterly instead of monthly, annually instead of semi-annually. A "balloon" loan is one in which the large part of the principal is not due until the maturity date, so that you keep more of the borrowed money longer. However, today it's more common for the lender to require repayment of principal and interest throughout the entire term of the loan.

Venture Capital   Even if you were turned down before when you attempted to receive venture capital, after you are established in business you can try again. Your presentation should give investors confidence in your business. Sell them the concept of your potential success; they are always looking for a winner. Send your proposal to a number of people, assuring them that you are over the difficult stage of getting established. Someone who is already in your kind of business will be a more understanding prospect. A week later, follow the mailing with a telephone call asking for a meeting.

Business Partner   Find an experienced partner who can take over part of the management, or a silent partner who will invest his money but have no voice in the business operation.

Manager   Find an experienced manager and give him a share of the business itself, or a share of its profits.

Part V
Appendices

Appendix A

The role of the computer

IN ORDER FOR THE ENTREPRENEUR TO UNDERSTAND BUSINESS BOOKKEEPING, accounting, and the importance of recordkeeping, the manual processing of such data and the bookkeeper's and accountant's roles have been described. Because of the minimal amount of data and the expense of other systems in a very small business, the manual system might be the only method that's used.

However, computers are rapidly taking over this area of operation even in small businesses. Caution may have been well-founded in years past regarding use of computerized information systems. They were easy to misuse. Many people were antagonized by them, particularly in the billing system. The early equipment was massive and expensive, and required specially trained and skilled operators. But progress has been rapid, and automated data processing has become much less expensive and considerably more tailored to the size of a business office. The computer is a tool, and like all other tools, has special capabilities—and liabilities.

It is the number of transactions and recordkeeping entries, and not the size of the business, that's significant in deciding whether to use manual methods or to buy or rent computer equipment, or to hire the services of companies that provide this assistance.

The computer and its uses

What is a computer and what are its uses? It's a machine but a person is needed to activate it. The computer receives data, stores it, recalls it, processes it according to instructions or human help, and prints or displays the results. It has the capacity to provide large amounts of information for decision-making.

The hardware—the computing machine and related equipment—performs the processing. Besides the computer itself, useful hardware includes disk drives—the machines which let the computer store and recall data from magnetic disks—and printers, which allow the computer to print data in "hard copy" form.

The programs are the software, usually purchased separately from the hardware and stored on disks, which direct the computer to do specific tasks. A large variety of programs are available to direct computers to handle diverse processing. One hardware system can do many different jobs, if provided with the proper software packages.

Speed and accuracy

Business management needs timely information in decision-making. Such information, often voluminous, must be accurate and immediately obtainable, and the recording should have been at minimal cost. Computers have two outstanding assets—they are fast and extremely accurate. This alone explains their value to business, and their cost should be weighed in light of time saved and improved efficiency of the business operation. In addition, creative use of the computer can allow the user to analyze data in useful ways that might be impossibly complex or time consuming if done manually.

Processing data

The true value lies in areas where there is considerable repetition of work—payroll processing, inventory recordkeeping, accounts receivable, and financial analysis. Some of the more frequent uses are also for processing data related to sales. Almost every step in retailing can benefit from data collection and processing and providing management with information needed for decision-making. Computerized billing systems are more accurate, faster, and cheaper than manual systems.

Software packages

It's the wide variety of available software packages, even more than the hardware, that opens up different possibilities to the business user. Some general-purpose software packages are useful to small businesses. One of the most popular types of software packages is the computerized spreadsheet, which allows you to design a format to your own specifications and store it in the computer. Data can then be entered and updated in this spreadsheet, and the computer performs all necessary calculations to provide totals. If one figure is changed or updated, all totals including that figure will automatically be corrected to reflect the change.

The database program

Another popular type of program is the database manager. Such a program allows you to enter and update almost any kind of data in the computer, which can then organize the data alphabetically, numerically, or by other methods, and print records based on the data. For instance, a business might enter a list of all suppliers, their addresses, and average amount of stock purchased from them each month. The computer could then print out a list of all suppliers in a certain area, or all suppliers providing more (or less) than a certain amount of stock each month.

Another use for the database manager is to maintain a mailing list. A retailer might create a database which consists of customers' names and addresses. The computer could then print out a mailing label for each customer, to be placed on a circular or other piece of mail. As in the prior example, the computer user could choose to print out mailing labels only for customers in a certain zip code, or only for customers who had made purchases since a certain date, if that information had been entered into the database.

The word processing package

Other software which the retailer might find useful are word processing packages, which allow the user to type whatever one might type on a typewriter, easily make corrections, and store the information in the computer or print it on the printer. Word processing produces neat and professional-looking correspondence; it also allows the retailer to store basic form letters and modify them as necessary for different uses, relieving him of the need to compose and type the letter each time it's needed. For example, a form letter designed to be sent to any customer who needs to be reminded to pay a bill might be stored in the computer. When the retailer wishes to send this letter to a customer, the name, address, and amount owed could be inserted into the form letter and printed out.

Software packages for the retailer

Other software packages are designed specifically for the retailer's special needs. Retail stores sell individual items directly to the customer. It's a problem for the retailer to keep track of every sale. It is difficult for the cashier or salesperson to write down every inventory item sold or returned, yet without this information it is difficult to monitor stock levels and determine when to reorder. Ultimately, the stock has to be counted, a slow and sometimes costly process; you can't afford to spend five cents to record a thirty-five cent purchase.

The practical computer software package to solve these problems for the retail store is called a POS—Point of Sale System. It eliminates most mental and manual tasks at the checkout counter. Supermarkets use such a system. The computer captures the data at point of sale. It records sales transactions, credit authorization, sales analysis, and accounts receivable. It provides tighter cash control and improves management because of inventory control.

For example, a customer buys an item and wishes to charge it to his account: The salesperson punches in the stock number of the item and the customer's account number. If the sale is accepted, the sales slip is printed with the desired detail, the item is deducted from inventory, and the amount of the sale is stored in the computer. If inventory of the purchased item drops too low, the computer notes this.

Selecting a computer system

Should you consider using a computer system, you must determine what will best meet your needs. Talk to users, and visit a number of computer retailers to see different combinations of hardware and software in action. Magazines and books designed for the business computer user are also available to help make your decision.

Remember that similar pieces of hardware and software packages of varying price, quality, and features are available from a wide range of manufacturers. If one software package seems too difficult or doesn't provide a feature you would like, another generally similar software package from a different company might prove more to your liking. The best software packages combine simplicity of use with flexibility that allows a business to adapt the software to its preferred system. In addition, if you have a specific need for a computer which no commercial software package meets, you might consider contracting a computer consulting firm to write software to your specifications.

Shall you buy the equipment, lease it, or hire the services of computer specialists? In the last option, data is supplied to a service bureau weekly, and trained operators produce the desired reports. For a small business, it may be efficient to do part of the recording manually and part by computer service. Using a computer service does not eliminate the need for the counsel of an accountant.

Computers vary as to types of input, processing, and output. Whether to buy or lease depends on monthly lease cost as compared with purchase and service costs, and also with all of the normal considerations when buying or leasing fixed assets. To go from manual to computer processing may require a new accounting system and also a qualified person to operate it.

When considering an inexpensive computer, determine whether it will do all you want it to do. Are you buying it for its usefulness now and also for its continued usefulness in a growing business? Counterbalance the cost of equipment with your ability to control inventory more effectively and to use data to better advantage in making management decisions. Fortunately, most computer systems can be adapted to perform larger or more complicated tasks with the addition of new software or hardware. You might begin with a less expensive hardware system and one software package, then add a disk drive with a larger storage capacity and more software packages, as your needs increase.

You can also have an expert come in and design a program for your particular operation, one that fits your needs and pocketbook.

Appendix B

The vocabulary of business

Accounts

Accounts payable—money owed to creditors.

Accounts receivable—money owed by customers.

Accruals Continually recurring short-term liabilities, e.g., accrual taxes.

Annuities Series of fixed-amount payments for a specified number of years.

Amortization Repayment of loan by installments.

Assets

Current assets—can be turned into cash within a year.

Fixed assets—are not replaced in less than a year; may include remodeling costs. Also called "capital assets."

Intangible assets—franchises, copyrights, patents, goodwill, and the like.

Balance Sheet Current financial statement, listing all assets and liabilities.

Balloon Payment When a debt is not fully amortized, the final payment is larger than the preceding payments.

Bill of Lading Written receipt by a carrier of goods listed and agreement to transport them to place and person specified.

Book Value Total assets minus total liabilities; may be different than true value because value of assets is as recorded. In a corporation, it is total book value divided by number of shares issued by the corporation.

Break-Even Point Amount of revenue from sales which exactly equals the amount of expense of operating the business. The number of units which must be sold at a specified price to cover fixed and variable expenses. Sales equal fixed expenses plus variable expenses. Break-even analysis is undertaken to determine level of sales at which a project's income would just equal costs; any units sold above break-even point contribute to the profit.

197

Capital   Money and other assets invested by owner. Capital investment covers fixed assets, inventory, working capital.

Cash-Flow Projection   Forecast of cash a business anticipates receiving and disbursing during the course of a given span of time, usually a month.

Caveat Emptor   "Let the buyer beware," a maxim expressing the rule that the buyer purchases at his peril.

Caveat Vendor   "Let the seller beware." It is the seller's duty to do what the ordinary man would do in a similar situation.

Chattel Mortgage   Mortgage on personal property.

Clayton Act   Prohibits certain practices if they tend to create a monopoly or lessen competition.

Collateral   Assets that are given as a security for a loan, to insure its repayment.

Commercial Bank   A bank of deposits with checking accounts, as distinguished from a savings bank.

Conditional Sales Contract   Paying for a purchase in installments; seller retains title until payment has been completed.

Consideration   A prerequisite for a contract that each party has incurred an obligation in exchange for the other party's also having done so. May be a deposit given in exchange for a promise.

Cost   Cost of sales, also cost of goods sold; affected by inventory shrinkage such as obsolescence. To determine cost of sales: beginning inventory plus purchases less ending inventory.
Direct cost—merchandise and whatever goes into the merchandise, whether product or service, e.g., freight.
Indirect cost—goods and services necessary to operate a business, e.g., interest on loan, price tags.
Fixed cost—costs that are incurred regardless of sales; does not change as volume of sales changes, e.g., rent.

Debit   The left-hand side of an account in an accounting ledger.

Deferred Charges   Prepaid expenses.

Deferred Income   A liability because the company is paid in advance and is liable to provide the service or item later.

Depreciation   Reduction in the book value of an asset over a period of time; it can be deducted from taxable income.

Earnings   Net profit after taxes.
Retained earnings—earnings not distributed to stockholders.

EBIT   Abbreviation for earnings before interest and taxes.

Equal Employment Opportunity Commission   Federal agency responsible for enforcing Civil Rights Act of 1984.

EPS   Abbreviation for earnings per share of stock after interest and taxes.

Equity   Company's net worth: the monetary value that exceeds claims against it.

Equity Financing   Raising funds by selling capital stock rather than incurring debt by borrowing.

Escrow   Placing with a third party assets that are to be released to a grantee upon fulfillment of a condition.

Expense All expenditures are not expenses, e.g., a truck may be an asset; expenses occur when expenditures are recorded so as to affect profits. Overhead expenses are operating expenses.

Factoring A financial institution buys a firm's accounts receivable and collects the debt.

Financial Ratios Yardsticks to compare operation of a business with that of other like businesses, and with one's own previous record, measuring liquidity, profitability, and performance.

Fiscal Year Period of twelve consecutive months chosen by a business as its accounting period.

FOB (Free-on-Board) Point at which title of goods transfers from vendor to buyer; it means title is transferred upon leaving premises of vendor and that shipping costs are paid by buyer.

Federal Trade Commission (FTC) Independent administrative agency that assists in enforcement of laws for maintaining free competition as basic to the federal economic system.

Goodwill Intangible assets of an established firm.

Gross Margin Gross margin is gross profit: If expressed in unit dollars, it is the number of units to be sold to break even; if expressed in percentages, the dollar volume to break even.

Formula

$$\frac{\text{fixed costs}}{\text{gross margin}} = \text{break-even point of sale}$$

Cost of sales − cost of goods sold = gross margin:

sales	$100,000
less cost of goods sold	60,000
gross margin	40,000
	40% mark-up
	100,000

Gross National Product (GNP) Measure of economic performance of the economy.

Holding Company Corporation operating for purpose of owning the common stock of other companies.

Implied Warranty Guarantee in contract law that implies that goods for sale are fit for a particular purpose.

Intrinsic Value Value justified by the fact; this distinguishes it from market price.

Inventory All items held for sale in the ordinary course of business, or in process of production for sale, or to be consumed in the production of goods for sale.
Inventory as collateral—analysis to determine its ability to be converted into cash.

Inventory financing—loans based on unsold inventory; the loan is paid when the goods are sold.

Inventory obsolescence—inventory no longer saleable.

Inventory shrinkage—almost unexplainable shrinkage, e.g., theft.

Jobber   Wholesaler or distributor.

Leverage   Use of external funds (not equity) to generate profit, e.g., borrowing funds at seven percent and making a net return on funds of twelve percent.

Liabilities   Accounts payable plus all costs of doing business. Contingent liabilities are those not recorded on the financial statement but which might become due, e.g., lawsuits.

Line of Credit   Arrangement by which a bank commits itself to lend up to a specified maximum amount of funds during a specified period; interest is paid only for the amount actually borrowed.

Liquidation   Discharge of all debts.

Chapter 11—business continues; creditors are protected; bank may appoint an examiner.

Chapter 13—a debt repayment plan over a period of time under court supervision and protection.

Liquidity   Firm's cash position and its ability to meet maturing obligations.

Loss Leader   Item priced at a loss or no profit, to attract customers.

Mark Down   Reduction in selling price.

Mark Up   Percentage change in price from purchase price to selling price.

National Brand   A producer's brand having wide distribution and popularity.

National Labor Relations Board (LRB)   Administrative board set up to protect labor's right to organize and bargain collectively.

Occupational Health and Safety Act (OSHA)   Act requiring that employers must use specific appliances and equipment for the safety of employees.

Owner's Equity   Assets less liabilities.

PE   Price-earnings ratio. Market price of share of stock divided by earnings (profit) per share.

Robinson-Patman Act   Amendment to the Clayton Act, giving the Federal Trade Commission authority to eliminate quantity discounts and other acts of discrimination.

Sherman Anti-Trust Act   First laws of Congress to preserve competition; outlawed monopolies and other acts in restraint of trade.

Stock Dividend   Dividend paid in additional shares of stock rather than cash.

Working Capital   To determine working capital, deduct current liabilities from current assets.

Appendix C

Equipment and depreciation

A LEDGER SHOULD BE KEPT ON EQUIPMENT, WITH A PAGE FOR EACH ITEM SHOWING model number, date of purchase, supplier, cost, number of check that paid for it, depreciation each year. List buildings (not land) and each item of equipment that is useful for a year or more; for example, furniture, automobiles, machinery, bookkeeping and other office equipment. Depreciation is taken on the expected life of items (for example, estimated life of an automobile is five years with depreciation of twenty percent a year). Small businesses usually charge depreciation at the end of their fiscal year, but a business with substantial fixed assets calculates depreciation monthly. For bookkeeping, a charge to expense is made to cover depreciation of fixed assets, and a corresponding credit is made to accumulated depreciation. Include sales tax and installation in the cost.

Appendix D

Rule of thumb formulas

Assets

liabilities plus capital

Break-even point

sales = fixed expenses + variable expenses

Cost of sales

beginning inventory + purchases − ending inventory

Price-earnings ratio (PE)

market price of share of stock divided by earnings (profit) per share

Working capital

current assets − current liabilities

Average percentage of mark up

cost of sales − cost of goods sold = gross margin (gross profit)

e.g., sales $100,000 − cost of goods sold $60,000 = $40,000

expressed as a percentage of sales, the mark up is computed by dividing gross margin by sales:

gross margin
sales $\quad \dfrac{\$40,000}{\$100,000} = 40\%$ mark up

Appendix E

Some non-bookkeeping records

Accounts Payable Journal
separate page for each vendor

Vendor

Address

Discount terms

Amount	Purchase Date	Returns & credits	Carrying charge	Due Amount	Payment Date	Check no.	Balance due

Accounts Receivable Journal
separate page for each charge account and lay away customer

Customer

Address
Charge

Lay away

Amount	Purchase Date	Returns & credits	Carrying charge	Due Amount	Payment Date	Balance due

Insurance Record

Insurer	Coverage	Premium Amount	Due date	Paid Amount	Date	Check no.

Capital Equipment
Typewriter

Model no.	Date of purchase	Manufacturer	Supplier	Cost*	Paid by check no.	Estimated life	Yearly** depreciation	Accumulated depr.	This year depr.

*Cost includes sales tax, installation fees.

**e.g., estimated life of a building is 20 years, with depreciation of 5% a year. If item was bought on contract, have columns for amount of down payment, monthly payments, balance due.

A column may be added for scrap value.

Postscript

I HOPE THAT THE BOOK HAS HELPED YOU BECOME A SUCCESSFUL ENTREPRENEUR. In my opening chapter I said it was not my purpose to assist you in procrastinating, should you decide you are equipped to be a good storekeeper.

You have done your homework. So now, what are you waiting for? Get to it! Good luck, as you *Open Your Own Shop*.

Index